Pork & Lamb

GENERAL EDITOR
CHUCK WILLIAMS

RECIPES
JOANNE WEIR

PHOTOGRAPHY
ALLAN ROSENBERG

TIME
LIFE
BOOKS

Time-Life Books is a division of Time Life Inc.
Time-Life is a trademark of Time Warner Inc. U.S.A.

President and CEO: John M. Fahey, Jr.
President, Time-Life Books: John D. Hall

TIME-LIFE CUSTOM PUBLISHING

Vice President and Publisher: Terry Newell
Sales Director: Frances C. Mangan
Editorial Director: Donia Steele

WILLIAMS-SONOMA
Founder/Vice-Chairman: Chuck Williams

WELDON OWEN INC.
President: John Owen
Publisher/Vice-President: Wendely Harvey
Associate Publisher: Laurie Wertz
Managing Editor: Lisa Chaney Atwood
Consulting Editor: Norman Kolpas
Copy Editor: Sharon Silva
Design: John Bull, The Book Design Company
Production Director: Stephanie Sherman
Production Editor: Janique Gascoigne
Co-Editions Director: Derek Barton
Co-Editions Production Manager (US): Tarji Mickelson
Food Photographer: Allan Rosenberg
Additional Food Photography: Allen V. Lott
Primary Food Stylist: Heidi Gintner
Assistant Food Stylist: Danielle Di Salvo
Prop Stylists: Danielle Di Salvo, Sandra Griswold
Glossary Illustrations: Alice Harth

The Williams-Sonoma Kitchen Library
conceived and produced by Weldon Owen Inc.
814 Montgomery St., San Francisco, CA 94133

In collaboration with Williams-Sonoma
3250 Van Ness Ave., San Francisco, CA 94109

Production by Mandarin Offset, Hong Kong
Printed in China

A Note on Weights and Measures:
All recipes include customary U.S. and metric
measurements. Metric conversions are based on
a standard developed for these books and have
been rounded off. Actual weights may vary.

A Weldon Owen Production

Copyright © 1995 Weldon Owen Inc.
Reprinted in 1995
All rights reserved, including the right of
reproduction in whole or in part in any form.

Library of Congress
Cataloging-in-Publication Data:

Weir, Joanne,
    Pork & lamb / general editor, Chuck Williams ;
    recipes, Joanne Weir ; photography, Allan Rosenberg.
        p.   cm. — (Williams-Sonoma kitchen library)
    Includes index.
    ISBN 0-7835-0309-1
    1. Cookery (Pork) 2. Cookery (Lamb and mutton)
    I. Williams, Chuck.   II. Title.   III. Title: Pork and lamb.   IV. Series.
TX749.5.P67W45   1995
641.6'63—dc20   94-48063
                                 CIP

Contents

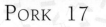

PORK 17

LAMB 63

INTRODUCTION

Traditionally, pork and lamb have been served only on special occasions: the English-style Sunday leg of lamb with its mint jelly, for example, or the glazed and clove-studded holiday ham.

I believe, however, that these two meats are ideal choices for everyday meals as well. Both cook up tender and delicious, their flavors offer welcome changes of pace and, best of all, when compared with other meats, they are amazingly healthful. Pork in particular is bred today so that it is almost as lean as skinless chicken breast.

If these few comments haven't sold you on trying pork and lamb, then I hope the rest of this volume will accomplish that task. The book begins with a review of all the basic information you'll need to prepare the meats, from simple kitchen equipment and guidelines for buying and storage to basic cooking techniques and recipes for preparing stock and accompaniments. These fundamentals are followed by 44 contemporary, easy-to-make recipes that reflect the impressive versatility of pork and lamb. Many of them feature the leaner cuts that cooks now wish to include in their home menus.

As you leaf through the following pages, let the full-color photograph that accompanies each recipe capture your imagination and inspire you to try one of these dishes—maybe even tonight. You are about to discover how pork and lamb can make any meal seem like a special occasion.

Chuck Williams

EQUIPMENT

A basic range of cookware and utensils to help you make a wide variety of pork and lamb dishes

Although pork and lamb are not the most common main-dish ingredients, their preparation calls for nothing in the way of specialized cooking equipment. A small array of everyday cookware and utensils is all you'll need to prepare every one of the recipes in this book.

A few of the items shown here, however, are particularly important. Good kitchen knives—with sharp stainless-steel blades and well-attached handles that feel comfortable and secure in your hand—will help you cut up ingredients efficiently and safely. And high-quality cookware will not only cook pork and lamb more successfully, but will also, for the relatively small investment in their purchase, last you a lifetime.

1. Baking Sheet
Sturdy metal sheet with raised rim for toasting nuts, drying bread crumbs and baking various foods such as spareribs and meatballs.

2. Assorted Kitchen Tools
Crockery jar holds rubber spatula for blending stuffing mixtures and smoothing meat loaves; wooden spoons for stirring and deglazing; wire whisk for stirring dressings and sauces; basting brush for basting roasted, grilled or broiled meats; metal spatula for turning burgers and other panfried, grilled, broiled or sautéed meats; slotted spoon for transferring small ingredients while draining off their cooking liquid or fat; and metal tongs for turning or transferring unwieldy ingredients.

3. Mixing Bowls
Sturdy bowls in graduated sizes for holding and mixing ingredients.

4. Roasting Pan and Rack
Heavy, durable metal pan large enough to hold good-sized roasts. Sturdy, stick-resistant metal rack facilitates lifting and turning, promotes even roasting and prevents roasts from sticking to pan.

5. Fine-Mesh Sieve
For straining solids from stock or other liquids.

6. Meat Loaf Pan

Stick-resistant, sturdy metal pan for shaping and baking meat loaves. Includes removable bottom that drains away fat during cooking.

7. Kitchen String

For tying stuffed and rolled slices of meat or holding larger cuts in compact shapes for even cooking. Choose good-quality linen string, which withstands intense heat with minimal charring.

8. Skewers

For holding together small pieces of meat during broiling or grilling. Before using wooden or bamboo skewers, soak in water for 30 minutes to prevent burning.

9. Frying Pan

Choose good-quality, heavy stainless steel, thick aluminum, cast iron or heavy enamel for rapid browning or frying. Sloped sides aid in the turning of meat and allow moisture to escape more easily for good browning.

10. Baking Dishes

Select heavy-duty glazed porcelain, stoneware, earthenware or glass for pork or lamb roasts or other oven-baked recipes.

11. Sauté Pan

For good browning of ingredients in the early stages of sautéing or braising, select a well-made heavy metal pan large enough to hold ingredients in a single layer without crowding. Straight sides about 2½ inches (6 cm) high help contain splattering. A close-fitting lid seals in moisture when ingredients are simmered.

12. Paring Knife

For peeling vegetables, cutting up small ingredients and doing other exacting work, such as cutting slits in chops for stuffing.

13. Carving Fork and Knife

Sturdy two-pronged fork steadies food during carving. Long, sturdy but flexible blade easily slices through large cuts of pork or lamb for serving.

14. Chef's Knife

All-purpose knife for chopping and slicing large items or large quantities of ingredients.

15. Meat Pounder

Heavy stainless-steel disk with sturdy handle, used to flatten boneless pieces of pork or lamb to be quickly sautéed or rolled and stuffed.

16. Cutting Board

For efficient cutting without damaging knives or kitchen counters, choose a good-sized cutting board made of sturdy hardwood or tough but resilient white acrylic.

17. Saucepan

For simmering sauces, glazes or other accompaniments for roasted, broiled (grilled) or panfried pork or lamb.

18. Pot Holder

Heavy-duty cotton provides good protection from hot cookware.

PORK BASICS

Guidelines to help you make the most of pork's noteworthy tenderness and flavor

Pork has undergone nothing short of a renaissance in recent years. Once regarded as a fatty meat to be shunned by the health-conscious, it has been gradually transformed by concerted breeding efforts into a relatively lean meat that averages just 6 grams of fat per 3-ounce (90-g) cooked serving. Add to that its other nutritional benefits as a rich source of protein, iron, zinc and B vitamins, not to mention its singularly sweet and mild flavor, and pork becomes a smart culinary choice indeed.

Of course, pork's leanness—like that of any source of animal protein—will depend on the part of the pig from which it comes. The leanest pork cuts are from the loin section, with the tenderloin the leanest of all. With careful attention to trimming off visible fat before cooking, and to removing liquid fat during cooking, many cuts of pork can be made to fit the requirements of a health-conscious diet. (For a guide to the pork cuts used in this book, see the glossary.)

GUIDELINES FOR BUYING AND STORING QUALITY PORK

Let common sense guide you in the purchase of pork. Begin by seeking out a good, reliable source, be it your local food store or a butcher shop.

Most pigs are slaughtered when barely more than 6 months old, and as a result their meat looks pale pink and fine in texture, their fat pure and white and any bones slightly reddish. If you see pork that looks coarse and has hard, white bones, chances are it comes from an older animal and should be avoided. Steer clear, as well, of any meat with an unpleasant odor. Good pork should smell clean and fresh.

As soon as you return home with your purchase, put the meat in the coldest part of the refrigerator, first loosening the wrapping to allow air to circulate freely. Use uncooked whole cuts or large pieces of pork within 3–4 days, and uncooked ground (minced) pork within 1–2 days. Leftover cooked pork should be refrigerated securely wrapped in plastic wrap or aluminum foil and eaten within 2 days.

Because pork is so tender, the uncooked meat is not a good candidate for freezing, which can diminish its texture, color and flavor. If you must freeze the meat, however, wrap it airtight in plastic freezer wrap or aluminum foil. It will keep for 3–6 months. Before cooking, thaw it in a refrigerator for 1–2 days, or in a microwave oven following the manufacturer's instructions.

BUTTERFLYING & STUFFING TENDERLOIN

Lean, tender and flavorful, a whole tenderloin is one of the most versatile cuts of pork. It can be cut crosswise into slices for cooking, or, as shown here, it can be butterflied—that is, split open and flattened—to be stuffed and cooked for a special occasion.

1. Splitting the tenderloin.
Using a chef's knife and steadying the tenderloin with your free hand, carefully cut a lengthwise slit along the center of the meat. As you cut, open the meat into 2 flaps, leaving them attached and cutting to within about ½ inch (12 mm) of the opposite side.

2. Pounding the meat.
Place the slit tenderloin on a work surface with its cut side up and the flaps open flat. Using a meat pounder, pound the tenderloin evenly all over until it has the uniform thickness called for in the recipe.

3. Tying the tenderloin.
Evenly arrange the prepared stuffing—here, roasted bell peppers—lengthwise along the center of the butterflied tenderloin. Wrap both sides around the stuffing and, using lengths of kitchen string, securely tie the stuffed tenderloin at regular intervals.

Pork Medallions with Lemon and Capers

Lamb Basics

Guidelines to help you enjoy lamb at its very best throughout the year

Lamb, like pork, provides not only culinary versatility, but also a wide variety of nutritional benefits, including protein, B vitamins, iron and zinc. Modern breeding of leaner animals has brought lamb well within the demands of today's healthier way of eating, particularly when the meat is balanced with high-carbohydrate, low-fat accompaniments. A 3-ounce (90-g) portion of cooked meat from the shank half of a leg of lamb, for example, contains only about 6 grams of fat and therefore derives barely more than one-third of its total 153 calories from fat. (For a guide to all the cuts of lamb used in this book, see the glossary.)

Guidelines for Buying and Storing Quality Lamb

Contrary to a popular misconception, lamb is not exclusively a springtime meat. Meat from any sheep younger than 1 year old qualifies as "genuine lamb," and active year-round breeding keeps it in constant supply in most food markets and butcher shops. That said, however, lamb purchased in late spring and early summer is more likely to come from younger animals and therefore to have the most tender texture and mild flavor of all. Meat from animals more than a year old is labeled "mutton"; it will have a notably stronger flavor and coarser texture, and is not suitable for the recipes in this book.

Although all lamb sold commercially will have been inspected for safety, about two-thirds of the lamb sold in the United States is also graded for quality. Prime is the best, most tender meat; it is followed by two grades: choice—the most widely available—and good.

Whatever lamb you buy, look for fresh-smelling, firm, pinkish red meat with pure white fat; any cut bones should appear moist, red and porous. Darker meat or dry, whiter bones could indicate mutton.

Store packages of lamb in the coldest part of the refrigerator with any wrappings loosened to allow air to circulate. Cook large pieces of lamb within 3–4 days, and ground (minced) lamb within 2 days of purchase. Wrapped airtight in plastic freezer wrap or aluminum foil, whole cuts of lamb may be frozen for up to 9 months, and ground lamb for no more than 4 months. Thaw the meat in the refrigerator for 1–2 days, or in a microwave oven.

Butterflied Leg of Lamb with Mint Mustard

Boning & Butterflying a Leg of Lamb

Boning and then butterflying a leg of lamb—that is, cutting flaps to open the meat out to a uniform thickness—makes it possible to cook the leg more evenly and quickly. A good-quality butcher should be able to do the job for you; but you also might like to try doing it yourself, using a sharp, sturdy, thin-bladed knife and following the steps shown here.

3. Removing the shank bone.
Grasp the shank bone at the top of the leg and cut through the ligaments around the bone. Then, keeping the knife blade against the bone, carefully cut the meat away from the bone. When you reach the shank bone's joint with the leg bone, cut through the ligaments and remove the shank bone.

1. Trimming the leg.
Before boning, chill the leg of lamb in the refrigerator for about 3 hours to firm up the meat for easier cutting. Using a thin-bladed knife, trim away the excess fat from the surface of the leg, carefully working parallel to the surface.

4. Removing the leg bone.
Cut down to the leg bone through the center of the meat. Cut around the joint at one end and ease the leg bone out of the meat. Holding the free joint, continue to cut and scrape down the length of the bone until it is free from the meat.

2. Removing the pelvic bone.
Locate the pelvic bone in the wide, rounded end, perpendicular to the length of the leg. With the pelvic bone end closest to you, gradually cut around the bone until you have exposed its ball-and-socket joint with the leg bone. Cut through the ligaments at the joint and pull the pelvic bone free.

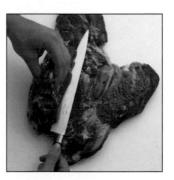

5. Butterflying the leg meat.
Holding the knife blade parallel to the work surface, cut into the thickest parts of the leg meat from the center outward toward the edge to open it out in a flap. Take care not to cut completely through the meat. The result should be a large, flat piece of meat of uniform thickness.

Cooking Techniques

Simple tips and hints to help you achieve the best results when cooking pork or lamb

Each of the pork and lamb recipes in this collection is complete unto itself, with no further instructions necessary. A grasp of the basic principles behind the cooking methods used throughout this book will, however, help you achieve the desired results with even greater ease.

Roasting

Cooking in an open pan in an oven's dry heat intensifies the flavor of such large, tender cuts of pork as crown roast, loin or ham, and such lamb cuts as the leg and the rack. To keep the meat moist and develop an attractively browned surface, baste the meat regularly with the pan juices or other liquid.

Use an instant-read thermometer to ensure that the meat reaches the desired internal temperature called for in the recipe. Bear in mind, however, that the interior temperature of a roast will continue to rise by up to 10°F (5°C) after you remove it from the oven to rest before carving.

Stir-frying

In this classic Chinese cooking technique, small, evenly cut pieces of meat and vegetables are rapidly stirred and tossed in a very hot pan coated with a thin film of oil. Traditionally, the half-spherical pan known as a wok is used, but a large, deep frying pan with sloped sides may be substituted. Meat is usually added to the pan immediately after such aromatics as ginger or garlic. Other ingredients are then added according to how long they take to cook, with the quickest cooking items added last.

Broiling & Grilling

The term *broiling* generally refers to cooking thinner, relatively tender cuts of meat beneath a dry heat source. For the best results, they are usually placed on a rack in a broiling pan, which is in turn placed under a broiler so that the top of the meat is 3–4 inches (7.5–10 cm) from the heat. The result should be nicely browned on the outside and still moist within.

Grilling produces similar results, using a bed of hot charcoals as its heat source, and the methods may be used interchangeably in most recipes. When grilling, take care to build the fire well enough in advance so the coals will be hot when you're ready to cook. For larger cuts of meat, add a few fresh coals to the fire before placing the meat on the grill, so the cooking temperature remains constant.

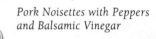

Pork Noisettes with Peppers and Balsamic Vinegar

BRAISING & STEWING

These two related cooking methods generally differ only in the size of the meat being cooked and the quantity of liquid in which they cook. Braising calls for larger pieces and relatively little liquid, and stewing applies to small, uniform pieces in a moderate amount of liquid. In either case, the meat is generally browned first in a little fat. Then, other solid ingredients and the liquid are added, the mixture is brought to a boil and promptly reduced to a gentle simmer, and the cooking vessel is covered and left to cook on the stove top or in the oven until the meat is tender.

Tougher cuts of meat, such as the leg or shoulder, are generally good choices for braising and stewing because they become more tender and flavorful with long, slow cooking.

SAUTÉING

A term derived from the French *sauter* ("to jump"), this method involves the searing or browning and quick cooking of tender, small or thin pieces of meat in a little fat. Vegetables may also be added, along with a liquid in which the ingredients simmer briefly until done—forming their own sauce. An important step in the preparation of any sautéed dish is deglazing—a term that refers to dissolving the rich, brown glaze of meat juices formed in the pan, thus adding their flavor to the finished dish.

1. Browning the meat.
In a sauté pan or frying pan large enough to hold the meat in a single layer without crowding, heat a thin layer of fat or oil as called for in the recipe. Add the meat— here, pork medallions—and cook until evenly browned on all sides.

2. Deglazing the pan.
Remove the meat from the pan. Over high heat, add the liquid called for in the recipe—here, white wine— and stir vigorously with a wooden spoon to dislodge and dissolve the browned bits from the pan bottom as the liquid comes to a boil.

Chicken Stock

One mistake that cooks sometimes make when preparing homemade chicken stock is adding too much water, thereby diluting the finished product. To make a highly flavorful chicken stock, add only enough water to cover the bones by 2 inches (5 cm) and then simmer the stock, uncovered, over very low heat. To save time in preparing the recipes in this book, purchased chicken stock may be substituted for this flavorful homemade variety.

5 lb (2.5 kg) chicken parts, such as backs, necks
   and wings, trimmed of excess fat
1 yellow onion, coarsely chopped
1 carrot, peeled and coarsely chopped
12 fresh parsley sprigs
pinch of dried thyme or fresh thyme leaves
1 bay leaf

*I*n a large saucepan or a stockpot, combine all the ingredients. Add water to cover by 2 inches (5 cm). Bring to a boil over high heat, then immediately reduce the heat to low. Simmer very gently, uncovered, until the stock tastes flavorful and the meat has fallen off the bones, 3–4 hours. Add water to the pan as needed to maintain the original level and skim off any scum that rises to the surface during cooking.

   Remove from the heat and strain through a fine-mesh sieve into a clean container. Place in the refrigerator and let cool completely. Lift off the fat that solidifies on the top and discard. Use immediately, or cover tightly and refrigerate for up to 3 days or freeze for up to 2 months.

Makes about 3 qt (3 l)

Herbed Bread Crumbs

This versatile recipe goes well with pork or lamb dishes. The best bread to use is a coarse-textured white bread that can be purchased sliced in 1- or 1½-pound (500- or 750-g) loaves. If the recipe calls for dried herbed bread crumbs, make the recipe as directed, then spread the crumbs on a baking sheet. Bake in a 325°F (165°C) oven, watching closely and stirring often to prevent over-browning during baking, until golden, about 5 minutes.

4 slices white bread
pinch of salt
pinch of freshly ground pepper
¼ teaspoon chopped fresh thyme or ⅛ teaspoon
   dried thyme
¼ teaspoon chopped fresh rosemary or ⅛ teaspoon
   dried rosemary

*C*ut the crusts off the bread and discard. Tear the bread into pieces. In a food processor fitted with the metal blade or in a blender, combine the bread, salt and pepper. Process the bread until it forms coarse crumbs.

   Add the thyme and rosemary and pulse a few times just until well mixed. Use immediately, or store in an airtight container in the freezer for up to 1 year.

Makes about 1 cup (2 oz/60 g)

Chicken Stock

Herbed Bread Crumbs

Plum and Ginger Chutney

Both Indian and English cooks take great pride in the making of chutneys—condiments based on fruits or vegetables cooked with sugar, vinegar and spices to form a jamlike consistency. This fragrant variety is a flavorful accompaniment to any pork or lamb dish. Any type of plum will work well.

¾ cup (6 fl oz/180 ml) cider vinegar
½ cup (3½ oz/105 g) firmly packed brown sugar
3 cloves garlic, minced
1 small yellow onion, minced
½ teaspoon ground cinnamon
3 tablespoons peeled and grated fresh ginger
¼ cup (2 oz/60 g) granulated sugar
2 lb (1 kg) plums, pitted and coarsely chopped

*I*n a nonaluminum saucepan over high heat, combine all the ingredients. Stir well and bring to a boil. Reduce the heat to low and simmer, uncovered, until the mixture thickens, 1½–2 hours.

Transfer to jars or other containers with tight-fitting lids, let cool, cover and refrigerate for up to 3 weeks.

Makes about 2 cups (1¼ lb/625 g)

Pear and Mustard Chutney

Most chutneys are simple to make and can be an excellent way to enjoy the bounty of the harvest. This one calls for crisp fall pears and gives both sweet and sour dimensions to foods. Use it with your favorite pork or lamb dishes.

6 large, firm but ripe pears, preferably Bosc or Comice, peeled, quartered and cored
¼ cup (2 oz/60 g) Meaux or other whole-grain mustard
¾ cup (6 fl oz/180 ml) white wine vinegar
½ cup (3½ oz/105 g) firmly packed brown sugar
½ cup (2½ oz/75 g) minced yellow onion
½ teaspoon ground cloves
½ teaspoon ground nutmeg
½ teaspoon ground allspice

*P*lace all of the ingredients in a bowl, stir well, cover and marinate overnight at room temperature.

The next day, transfer the mixture to a nonaluminum saucepan and bring to a boil. Reduce the heat to low and simmer, uncovered, until the mixture thickens, 1½–2 hours.

Transfer to jars or other containers with tight-fitting lids, let cool, cover and refrigerate for up to 3 weeks.

Makes about 2 cups (1¼ lb/625 g)

Plum and Ginger Chutney

Pear and Mustard Chutney

15

Baked Ham with Maple-Pineapple Glaze

½ partially boned country-style cured ham, 6–7 lb (3–3.5 kg), such as Virginia
30 whole cloves
½ cup (4 fl oz/125 ml) pineapple juice
3 tablespoons maple syrup
3 tablespoons brown sugar

An old-fashioned country ham, punctuated with cloves and glazed to a rich mahogany color, always makes a memorable meal. The flavors are a gentle, pleasant mix of sweet and salty. You should try to buy the best ham possible, preferably one that has been dry-cured with salt and sugar and then lightly smoked.

Rinse the ham well in several changes of cold water. Place in a large bowl, add water to cover completely and refrigerate overnight.

Remove the ham from the water and discard the water. Pat the ham dry. Place in a roasting pan. Using a sharp knife, remove the skin and slice off enough fat so that a layer only ½ inch (12 mm) thick remains. Score the ham fat with crisscrosses to form a diamond pattern. Stick a clove in each diamond.

Preheat an oven to 325°F (165°C).

In a small saucepan over medium heat, combine the pineapple juice, maple syrup and brown sugar and stir until the sugar dissolves, about 1 minute. Brush the surface of the ham with some of the glaze and place the ham in the oven.

Bake, basting every 30 minutes with the remaining glaze, until the ham is golden brown and a thick glaze has formed on the surface, 2–2½ hours. Remove from the oven, cover lightly with aluminum foil and let rest for 30 minutes before carving.

To serve, cut the ham into slices and arrange on a warmed platter or individual plates. Serve at once.

Serves 8–10

Grilled Pork Tenderloin with Dried-Fruit Chutney

FOR THE DRIED-FRUIT CHUTNEY:

6 tablespoons (3 fl oz/90 ml) balsamic
  vinegar

½ cup (3½ oz/105 g) firmly packed
  brown sugar

¼ lb (125 g) dried apricots

¼ lb (125 g) dried pitted prunes

¼ lb (125 g) dried cranberries

1 teaspoon grated orange zest

juice of 1 orange

½ cup (4 fl oz/125 ml) brewed orange
  spice tea

¼ teaspoon ground cinnamon

¼ teaspoon ground allspice

3 pork tenderloins, about ¾ lb (375 g)
  each, trimmed of excess fat

2 tablespoons vegetable oil

salt and freshly ground pepper

Chutney and pork are natural partners. For this recipe, try using dried apples, cherries or figs for any of the dried fruits. Or, substitute the dried-fruit chutney with one made of fresh fruit and spices (recipe on page 15). For another variation, try lapsang souchong tea instead of orange spice to give the chutney a smoky flavor that pairs well with the grilled pork. Serve this dish with steamed rice and grilled vegetables or simply garnish with thin strips of orange peel and a fresh herb sprig.

To make the chutney, in a saucepan, combine the vinegar, sugar, apricots, prunes, cranberries, orange zest and juice, tea, cinnamon and allspice. Bring to a boil over medium heat, stirring occasionally, then reduce the heat to low. Simmer gently, uncovered, until thick, 1–2 hours, adding water as necessary to prevent sticking. Remove from the heat and let cool to room temperature.

Prepare a fire in a charcoal grill.

Brush the pork tenderloins with the vegetable oil and season to taste with salt and pepper. Place the tenderloins on the grill rack 4 inches (10 cm) from the heat source and grill, turning occasionally, until golden brown on all sides, firm to the touch, and pale pink when cut in the thickest portion, about 12 minutes.

Remove the tenderloins from the grill and cover with aluminum foil. Let rest for 2–3 minutes before carving. Cut crosswise into slices ½ inch (12 mm) thick. Place 4 or 5 slices on each plate along with a spoonful of chutney. Serve immediately.

Serves 6

Sausage and White Bean Stew

1½ cups (10½ oz/330 g) dried small white (navy) or Great Northern beans

1 small yellow onion, quartered, plus 1 medium-sized yellow onion, minced

¼ teaspoon ground allspice

¼ teaspoon ground cloves

6 cups (48 fl oz/1.5 l) chicken stock (recipe on page 14)

¼ cup (2 fl oz/60 ml) olive oil

1 red bell pepper (capsicum), seeded, deribbed and cut into ½-inch (12-mm) dice

4 cloves garlic, minced

6 sweet pork sausages, about 1½ lb (750 g) total weight, pricked with a fork

salt and freshly ground pepper

This recipe can be made ahead of time and then reheated just before serving. Other dried beans—pinto beans, kidney beans, chick-peas (garbanzo beans) or black beans—can be substituted, although cooking times will vary according to the type you choose. Garnish with chopped parsley or freshly grated Parmesan cheese, if you like. Serve with toasted slices of country-style bread rubbed with garlic and brushed with extra-virgin olive oil.

*P*ick over the beans and discard any stones; rinse well. Place in a bowl and add water to cover generously. Soak for at least 4 hours or as long as overnight.

Drain the beans and place them in a saucepan. Add the quartered onion, allspice, cloves, chicken stock and water to cover by 3 inches (7.5 cm). Bring to a boil over high heat, reduce the heat to medium-low and simmer, uncovered, until the beans are tender, 30–40 minutes. Remove the quartered onion and discard. Set the beans aside.

In a large sauté pan over medium heat, warm the olive oil. Add the minced onion, bell pepper, garlic and sausages and cook, stirring occasionally, until the onion is very soft, about 10 minutes. Add the beans and their liquid and bring to a boil. Reduce the heat to low and simmer gently, uncovered, until the liquid has thickened, 30–40 minutes. Season to taste with salt and pepper.

To serve, remove the sausages from the pan and cut on the diagonal into thin slices. Return the slices to the pan and heat thoroughly. Spoon into warmed bowls and serve immediately.

Serves 6

Pork Sausage Sandwich with Red and Yellow Peppers

2 tablespoons extra-virgin olive oil

1 large red (Spanish) onion, cut into wedges ½ inch (12 mm) wide

1 yellow bell pepper (capsicum), seeded, deribbed and cut lengthwise into strips ½ inch (12 mm) wide

2 red bell peppers (capsicums), seeded, deribbed and cut lengthwise into strips ½ inch (12 mm) wide

¼ cup (2 fl oz/60 ml) water

4 spicy pork sausages, about 1 lb (500 g) total weight, pricked with a fork

12 slices rustic country-style bread

2 cloves garlic

¼ cup (2 fl oz/60 ml) mayonnaise

These sandwiches can also be topped with fresh basil leaves, grilled or broiled eggplant (aubergine) slices and melted Fontina cheese.

In a large frying pan or sauté pan over medium heat, warm the olive oil. Add the onion wedges and sauté, stirring occasionally, until they begin to soften, about 5 minutes. Add the yellow and red bell peppers and continue to cook uncovered, stirring occasionally, until the peppers are soft, about 10 minutes. Transfer the peppers and onions to a platter and keep warm.

Place the same pan over medium heat and add the water. Then add the sausages and cook, turning occasionally, until cooked through, about 12 minutes.

While the sausages are cooking, toast the bread.

Transfer the sausages to a cutting surface and cut on the diagonal into slices ¼ inch (6 mm) thick.

Rub one side of each toasted slice with the whole garlic cloves, holding the toast as if it were a flat hand-held grater and moving the garlic back and forth over it. Spread the garlic-rubbed side of half of the bread slices with a thin layer of mayonnaise. Divide the sausage slices, peppers and onions evenly among the bread slices. Top with the remaining toasted slices, garlic-rubbed side down.

Place the sandwiches on individual plates. Cut them in half on the diagonal and serve immediately.

Serves 6

Pork Verde Burritos

2 tablespoons vegetable oil

2 lb (1 kg) boneless pork shoulder or butt, trimmed of excess fat and cut into 1-inch (2.5-cm) cubes

2 yellow onions, chopped

3 large green bell peppers (capsicums), seeded, deribbed and cut into ½-inch (12-mm) dice

1 or 2 fresh jalapeño chili peppers, seeded and minced

5 cloves garlic, minced

1½ tablespoons ground cumin

4 lb (2 kg) tomatillos, husks removed, seeded, chopped and drained (4 cups/1½ lb/750 g)

1 cup (1 oz/30 g) chopped fresh cilantro (fresh coriander)

1 cup (8 fl oz/250 ml) water

6 large flour tortillas

1 avocado, halved, pitted, peeled and thinly sliced

Accompany these burritos with bowls of sour cream, chopped green (spring) onions, fresh cilantro leaves, lime wedges, and store-bought or homemade tomatillo salsa for each person to add as they like.

*I*n a large, heavy pot over medium-high heat, warm the vegetable oil. Working in batches if necessary, add the pork cubes in a single layer (do not crowd the pan) and brown on all sides, 10–12 minutes. Using a slotted spoon, transfer the pork to a plate.

Reduce the heat to medium and add the onions, bell peppers and chili peppers. Sauté, stirring occasionally, until the onions are very soft, about 10 minutes. Add the garlic and cumin and continue to sauté, stirring, for 1 minute. Add the tomatillos, cilantro and water and then return the pork to the pot. Bring to a boil, reduce the heat to low, cover and simmer until the pork is very tender when pierced with a fork and the mixture is very thick, 1½–2 hours.

Preheat an oven to 300°F (150°C). Wrap the tortillas tightly in aluminum foil. Heat them in the oven until hot, about 15 minutes.

One at a time, place one-sixth of the hot filling in the center of each warm tortilla and top with one-sixth of the avocado slices. Roll up the tortillas to enclose the filling, leaving the ends open. Place on individual plates and serve immediately.

Serves 6

Barbecued Spareribs

6 lb (3 kg) pork spareribs in 2 racks,
    trimmed of excess fat
salt and freshly ground pepper

FOR THE BARBECUE SAUCE:
1 tablespoon vegetable oil
1 small yellow onion, minced
1 cup (8 fl oz/250 ml) tomato purée
3 tablespoons Dijon-style mustard
¼ cup (2 fl oz/60 ml) fresh lemon juice
¼ cup (2 oz/60 g) firmly packed
    brown sugar
2 tablespoons Worcestershire sauce
2 tablespoons hot-pepper sauce, such
    as Tabasco
¼ teaspoon ground allspice
¼ teaspoon ground ginger
¼ cup (2 fl oz/60 ml) water
salt and freshly ground pepper

Finishing the cooking of ribs over a mesquite fire gives them a smoky flavor. During the grilling, watch the ribs closely, turning them to ensure even browning and removing them as soon as they are browned nicely. Serve with corn on the cob and coleslaw.

Preheat an oven to 350°F (180°C).

Arrange the spareribs in a single layer on a baking sheet. Season well with salt and pepper; cover with aluminum foil. Bake until tender when pierced with a fork, 1¼–1½ hours.

Prepare a fire in a charcoal grill, preferably using mesquite charcoal.

Meanwhile, make the barbecue sauce: In a saucepan over medium heat, warm the vegetable oil. Add the onion and sauté, stirring occasionally, until very soft, about 10 minutes. Add the tomato purée, mustard, lemon juice, brown sugar, Worcestershire sauce, hot-pepper sauce, allspice, ginger, water, and salt and pepper to taste. Bring to a boil, reduce the heat to low and simmer gently, uncovered, until the sauce thickens, 5–10 minutes. Remove from the heat.

Remove the ribs from the oven and discard the foil. Place the ribs on the grill rack 5 inches (13 cm) from the heat source and brush with the barbecue sauce. Cover the grill partially and cook the ribs until they are browned on the first side, 5–10 minutes. Turn over the ribs, baste them with additional sauce, cover partially, and continue to cook on the second side until golden brown, 5–10 minutes.

Remove from the grill and serve immediately.

Serves 6

Red Onions Stuffed with Pork

¼ cup (1¼ oz/37 g) pine nuts
salt to taste, plus ¾ teaspoon salt
6 large red (Spanish) onions
freshly ground pepper
½ lb (250 g) ground (minced) lean pork
½ cup (3½ oz/105 g) long-grain white
   rice, rinsed and drained
¼ cup (1½ oz/45 g) golden raisins
   (sultanas)
½ cup (3 oz/90 g) peeled, seeded and
   chopped tomatoes (fresh or canned)
1 tablespoon tomato paste
¼ cup (½ oz/15 g) fresh chopped
   parsley, preferably flat-leaf (Italian)
2 tablespoons chopped fresh mint, plus
   fresh mint leaves for garnish
¼ teaspoon ground allspice
2 tablespoons olive oil
1 cup (8 fl oz/250 ml) chicken stock,
   or as needed (recipe on page 14)
½ lemon

This stuffing can also be made with lamb, and either stuffing can be used to fill red, green or yellow bell peppers (capsicums).

Preheat an oven to 350°F (180°C). Spread the pine nuts on a baking sheet and bake, shaking the pan occasionally, until lightly golden, 3–5 minutes. Remove from the oven and let cool. Raise the oven temperature to 375°F (190°C).

Meanwhile, bring a large saucepan three-fourths full of water to a boil and add salt to taste. Add the onions and boil for 15 minutes to cook partially. Drain well and let cool. Cut a ½-inch (12-mm) slice off the top of each onion. Trim a slice just thick enough off the bottom of each onion so that it will stand upright; do not trim too much or the onion will fall apart. Using a small knife, cut the center out of each onion, leaving a shell ½ inch (12 mm) thick. Discard the removed onion or reserve for another use. Season the onion shells with salt and pepper to taste.

In a bowl, combine the pork, toasted pine nuts, rice, raisins, tomatoes, tomato paste, parsley, chopped mint, allspice, olive oil, the ¾ teaspoon salt, and pepper to taste. Mix well. Stuff the onions with this mixture, no more than three-fourths full to allow room for expansion. Place the onions close together in a baking dish. In a small saucepan, bring the 1 cup (8 fl oz/250 ml) chicken stock to a boil and pour it between the onions. Squeeze the lemon half evenly over the onion tops. Cover with aluminum foil and bake until the onions are tender when pierced with a knife and the rice is cooked, 45–50 minutes. Add more stock to the baking dish as needed.

Carefully transfer the onions to a platter and pour the pan juices over the filling. Let cool slightly, then garnish with the mint leaves. Serve warm.

Serves 6

Winter Casserole of Pork, Sauerkraut and Potatoes

1 can (27 oz/845 ml) sauerkraut,
   drained
4 cups (32 fl oz/1 l) water
1 firm green apple, such as Granny
   Smith or pippin, halved, cored,
   peeled and coarsely grated
2 cups (16 fl oz/500 ml) chicken stock
   (recipe on page 14)
freshly ground pepper
1½ lb (750 g) boneless pork loin,
   trimmed of excess fat and cut into
   slices ¼ inch (6 mm) thick
3 teaspoons vegetable oil
2 lb (1 kg) red potatoes, unpeeled,
   cut into slices ⅛ inch (3 mm) thick
1 yellow onion, thinly sliced
salt

This main course recipe is inspired by a traditional Alsatian dish called beckenoffe, *or "baker's oven," a slowly baked French casserole.*

Place the sauerkraut in a colander and pour the water over it. Drain well, shaking the colander to remove any excess water.

In a saucepan over high heat, combine the sauerkraut, apple, 1½ cups (12 fl oz/375 ml) of the chicken stock and pepper to taste. Bring to a boil, then immediately reduce the heat to low. Simmer, uncovered, until the sauerkraut softens, about 30 minutes. Remove from the heat and drain in a colander. Set the sauerkraut aside.

Preheat an oven to 350°F (180°C). Working with 1 pork loin slice at a time, place it between 2 sheets of plastic wrap. Using a meat pounder, pound the pork gently until it is evenly ⅛ inch (3 mm) thick. In a large frying pan over medium heat, warm 2 teaspoons of the vegetable oil. Working in batches if necessary, fry the pork slices, turning once, until white, about 1 minute on each side. Remove from the pan and set aside.

Rub a 13-by-9-inch (33-by-23-cm) baking dish with the remaining 1 teaspoon oil. Layer all the potato slices on the bottom of the dish. Cover with the onion slices, and then with the pork slices. Pour the remaining ½ cup (4 fl oz/125 ml) stock evenly over the top. Arrange the drained sauerkraut over the pork. Cover with aluminum foil and bake until the pork and potatoes are tender when pierced with a fork, 1–1¼ hours.

To serve, remove the foil and season to taste with salt. Spoon onto individual plates and serve at once.

Serves 6

Pork Noisettes with Peppers and Balsamic Vinegar

1 red bell pepper (capsicum), roasted
   and peeled *(see glossary, page 104)*
1 yellow bell pepper (capsicum), roasted
   and peeled *(see glossary, page 104)*
2 tablespoons balsamic vinegar
salt and freshly ground pepper
3 pork tenderloins, about ¾ lb (375 g)
   each, trimmed of excess fat
2 tablespoons olive oil
2 cups (16 fl oz/500 ml) chicken stock
   (recipe on page 14)
⅓ cup (2 oz/ 60 g) Niçoise or Kalamata
   olives, pitted
fresh thyme sprigs

Serve this dish as a main course, accompanied with oven-roasted red potatoes cooked with garlic cloves and chopped rosemary and thyme.

Cut the roasted bell peppers lengthwise into strips ¾ inch (2 cm) wide. Place in a bowl and add 1 tablespoon of the balsamic vinegar and salt and pepper to taste. Toss well.

Butterfly the pork tenderloins by making a long slit down the length of each tenderloin, cutting just deep enough so that the tenderloin opens up to lay flat; be careful not to cut all the way through (see page 9). Flatten the tenderloins and pound gently with a meat pounder. Season with salt and pepper. Place the pepper strips side by side down the center of each pork tenderloin. Close up the tenderloins and, using kitchen string, tie the loins at 1-inch (2.5-cm) intervals so that they assume their original shape.

In a large frying pan or sauté pan over medium-high heat, warm the olive oil. Add the pork and brown on all sides, about 5 minutes total. Reduce the heat to medium-low, cover and continue to cook slowly, turning occasionally, until the meat is firm to the touch and pale pink when cut in the thickest portion, 15–18 minutes. Transfer the tenderloins to a platter, cover with aluminum foil and keep warm. Increase the heat to high and add the chicken stock, the remaining 1 tablespoon balsamic vinegar and the olives to form a sauce. Cook, stirring occasionally, until reduced by half, about 5 minutes.

Snip the strings on the tenderloins and discard. Cut the meat crosswise into slices 1 inch (2.5 cm) thick. To serve, arrange the pork slices on warmed plates and spoon the sauce over them. Garnish with the thyme sprigs and serve immediately.

Serves 6

Apricot-Glazed Pork Kebabs with Wild Rice

¼ cup (2 oz/60 g) unsalted butter

6 tablespoons fresh orange juice

1 tablespoon peeled and grated or minced fresh ginger

1 jar (10 oz/315 g) apricot preserves

1½ lb (750 g) pork tenderloin, trimmed of excess fat and cut into 1-inch (2.5-cm) cubes

salt to taste, plus ¾ teaspoon salt

freshly ground pepper

1¼ cups (7½ oz/235 g) wild rice, rinsed and drained

4 cups (32 fl oz/1 l) water

½ cup (3 oz/90 g) dried apricot halves

fresh parsley sprigs, preferably flat-leaf (Italian)

A double dose of apricots lends a mild and fruity sweetness to this savory dish.

*I*n a small saucepan over medium heat, combine the butter, orange juice, ginger and apricot preserves. When the butter and preserves melt and the mixture begins to bubble around the edges in 3–4 minutes, transfer it to a bowl. Let cool for 10 minutes.

Season the pork cubes with salt and pepper to taste and add them to the apricot preserves mixture. Stir to coat evenly. Let stand at room temperature for 30 minutes.

Meanwhile, if using bamboo skewers, soak 12 of them in water to cover for 30 minutes. Place the wild rice, ¾ teaspoon salt and the water in a saucepan. Bring to a boil, reduce the heat to low, cover and cook for 20 minutes. Uncover, stir in the dried apricots, re-cover and continue to cook until the rice is tender, about 25 minutes longer. Check from time to time and, if necessary to prevent sticking, add a little water. When the rice is ready, fluff it with a fork.

While the rice is cooking, prepare a fire in a charcoal grill, or preheat a broiler (griller). Drain the bamboo skewers, if using, and thread the pork cubes on the bamboo or 12 metal skewers, dividing evenly. Reserve the excess apricot marinade. Fifteen minutes before the rice is ready, place the skewers on the grill rack or on the rack of a broiler pan. Grill or broil 4 inches (10 cm) from the heat source, turning occasionally and basting with the reserved glaze, until the pork is browned and firm to the touch, 10–12 minutes.

To serve, place 2 skewers on each plate and accompany with the wild rice. Garnish with parsley and serve immediately.

Serves 6

Roast Loin of Pork with Baked Apples

1 boneless pork loin, about 3 lb
  (1.5 kg), trimmed of excess fat
2 cloves garlic, minced
1 tablespoon chopped fresh rosemary
½ teaspoon salt, plus salt to taste
freshly ground pepper
6 firm green apples, such as pippin
  or Granny Smith
¼ cup (2 oz/60 g) firmly packed
  brown sugar
2 tablespoons unsalted butter
½ cup (4 fl oz/125 ml) water
¼ teaspoon ground cinnamon
½ teaspoon grated lemon zest

For a more substantial main course, serve the pork and baked apples alongside scalloped potatoes (see recipe on page 46; omit the ham and prepare half a recipe of the potatoes).

*P*osition a rack in the bottom part of the oven and preheat to 500°F (260°C).

Place the pork on a rack in a roasting pan. In a small bowl, mix together the garlic, rosemary, the ½ teaspoon salt, and pepper to taste. Rub the mixture evenly over the surface of the pork. Place in the oven and roast until the pork loin begins to spatter, about 15 minutes.

Meanwhile, peel the top one-third of each apple and then core the apples. In a small pan, combine the sugar, butter, water, cinnamon and lemon zest and bring to a boil, stirring.

Reduce the oven temperature to 350°F (180°C). At the same time, place the apples in a 2-qt (2-l) baking dish and pour the syrup evenly over them. Cover the dish with aluminum foil and place in the oven with the pork. Continue to roast the pork until an instant-read thermometer inserted into the center of the loin registers 150°F (66°C) or the meat is pale pink when cut in the thickest portion, about 30 minutes longer. Cook the apples until tender when pierced with a fork, 20–25 minutes. Remove the pork and the apples from the oven. Cover the pork with aluminum foil and let rest for 10 minutes before carving. Keep the apples warm.

Slice the pork and arrange on a warmed serving platter with the baked apples. Drizzle the juices from the dish that held the apples over the pork and the apples. Serve immediately.

Serves 6

Thai Pork Satay with Peanut Sauce

1½ teaspoons curry powder
¼ cup (2 fl oz/60 ml) coconut milk
salt
1 lb (500 g) boneless pork loin,
   trimmed of excess fat and cut into
   strips 3 inches (7.5 cm) long by
   1 inch (2.5 cm) wide by ⅛ inch
   (3 mm) thick

FOR THE PEANUT SAUCE:
½ cup (3 oz/90 g) unsalted roasted
   peanuts
1 cup (8 fl oz/250 ml) coconut milk
1 tablespoon brown sugar
⅛–¼ teaspoon crushed red pepper
   flakes
2 teaspoons fish sauce
3 teaspoons rice vinegar or cider vinegar
salt

fresh cilantro (fresh coriander) leaves

Serve this dish as a first course or double the recipe and offer as a main course. A perfect accompaniment is thinly sliced cucumbers and red onion dressed with rice vinegar lightly sweetened with sugar and seasoned with minced fresh chili pepper. The coconut milk and fish sauce can be found in Asian markets and well-stocked food stores.

*I*n a bowl, combine the curry powder, coconut milk, salt to taste and the pork. Stir to coat the pork evenly with all the ingredients. Cover and refrigerate for 1 hour.

Meanwhile, soak 18 bamboo skewers in water to cover for 30 minutes. To make the sauce, in a food processor fitted with the metal blade or in a blender, process the peanuts to a coarse meal. Add the coconut milk, brown sugar, red pepper flakes, fish sauce, vinegar and salt to taste and process to combine. Pour into a frying pan and place over medium heat. Bring to a simmer and cook until the sauce is thick, about 10 minutes. Remove from the heat and place in a small bowl.

Preheat a broiler (griller).

Drain the skewers and thread the pork strips onto them. Arrange the skewers on a baking sheet and slip under the broiler 4 inches (10 cm) from the heat source. Broil (grill), turning occasionally, until the pork is cooked through, 2–3 minutes total.

Transfer the skewers to a warmed platter, garnish with the cilantro and spoon the peanut sauce evenly over the top. Serve immediately.

Serves 6

Pork Medallions with Lemon and Capers

2 pork tenderloins, about ¾ lb (375 g)
  each, trimmed of excess fat
½ cup (2½ oz/75 g) all-purpose
  (plain) flour
salt and freshly ground pepper
about 4 tablespoons olive oil
4 cloves garlic, minced
½ teaspoon chopped fresh rosemary
½ cup (4 fl oz/125 ml) dry white wine
2 cups (16 fl oz/500 ml) chicken stock
  (recipe on page 14)
¼ cup (2 oz/60 g) drained capers,
  rinsed
1–2 tablespoons fresh lemon juice
lemon wedges

Pork medallions cook in a few minutes and make an impressive main course. Serve this dish with potatoes that have been roasted with a little fresh lemon juice, olive oil and fresh rosemary.

Cut the tenderloins crosswise into slices ½ inch (12 mm) thick. Place each slice between 2 sheets of plastic wrap and, using a meat pounder, pound the pork gently until it is evenly ¼ inch (6 mm) thick.

On a plate, combine the flour and salt and pepper to taste. In a large frying pan or sauté pan over medium-high heat, warm 2 tablespoons of the olive oil. Coat the pork with the seasoned flour, shaking off the excess. Working in batches, add the pork to the pan in a single layer and sauté, turning once, until golden brown, 1½–2 minutes on each side. Transfer to a platter and keep warm. Continue with the remaining pork, adding the remaining olive oil if needed. Transfer the remaining pork to the platter and keep warm.

Reduce the heat to low, add the garlic and rosemary and sauté, stirring, for 30–60 seconds. Raise the heat to high, add the wine and deglaze the pan by stirring to dislodge any browned bits on the pan bottom. Boil until reduced by half, about 1 minute. Add the chicken stock and again boil until reduced by half, about 5 minutes. Stir in the capers, lemon juice, and salt and pepper to taste.

Pour the sauce over the pork and garnish with the lemon wedges. Serve immediately.

Serves 6

Stuffed Pork Chops with Prunes and Apples

15 pitted prunes

boiling water, as needed

2 tablespoons unsalted butter

1 yellow onion, minced

1 large firm green apple, such as
   Granny Smith or pippin, peeled,
   halved, cored and coarsely grated

1 cup (2 oz/60 g) fresh herbed bread
   crumbs *(recipe on page 14)*

pinch of ground cinnamon

salt and freshly ground pepper

6 center-cut pork chops, each about
   6 oz (185 g) and 1 inch (2.5 cm)
   thick, trimmed of excess fat

2 tablespoons vegetable oil

The basic elements of a stuffing for pork chops are butter, onion and bread crumbs, but mixed fresh herbs, minced garlic, sautéed chopped wild mushrooms, or chopped cooked bacon can also be added, if you like. For a beautiful presentation, serve on a bed of steamed and julienned vegetables.

*P*lace the prunes in a bowl and pour in boiling water to cover. Let stand for 30 minutes. Drain the prunes well and chop finely. Set aside.

In a frying pan over medium heat, melt the butter. Add the onion and sauté, stirring occasionally, until very soft, about 10 minutes. Transfer the onion to a bowl and add the apple, bread crumbs, cinnamon, prunes, and salt and pepper to taste. Mix well.

Using a small, sharp knife, cut a horizontal slit 1 inch (2.5 cm) long into the side of each pork chop. Continuing to use the knife, work inward from the slit, cutting almost to the opposite side of the chop; be careful not to cut through the chop completely. Stuff an equal amount of the stuffing into each chop; flatten the chops slightly.

In a frying pan large enough to hold the chops in a single layer without crowding, warm the vegetable oil over medium heat. Add the chops and cook, uncovered, for 5 minutes. Turn the chops over and season to taste with salt and pepper. Reduce the heat to medium-low and continue to cook, uncovered, turning occasionally, until golden and firm to the touch, about 12 minutes longer.

Transfer to warmed plates and serve immediately.

Serves 6

Pork Meat Loaf with Sweet-and-Hot Sauce

2 tablespoons unsalted butter

12 green (spring) onions, including tender green tops, thinly sliced

¼ lb (125 g) fresh mushrooms, thinly sliced

½ cup (1 oz/30 g) fresh herbed bread crumbs (recipe on page 14)

1 lb (500 g) ground (minced) lean pork

½ lb (250 g) ground (minced) lean beef

1 egg, lightly beaten

1 clove garlic, minced

3 tablespoons chopped fresh parsley, preferably flat-leaf (Italian)

¼ cup (2 fl oz/60 ml) chicken stock (recipe on page 14)

1 teaspoon salt

freshly ground pepper

FOR THE SWEET-AND-HOT SAUCE:

⅓ cup (3 fl oz/80 ml) prepared ketchup or tomato sauce

½ cup (4 oz/125 g) sugar

⅓ cup (3 fl oz/80 ml) water

⅓ cup (3 fl oz/80 ml) white wine vinegar

1 tablespoon soy sauce

½ teaspoon cayenne pepper

1½ tablespoons cornstarch mixed with 3 tablespoons cold water

Serve this pork meat loaf with creamy mashed potatoes and steamed green beans. If you have any meat loaf left over, tuck it into sandwiches with sliced Cheddar cheese and tomatoes, or carry it along on a picnic for serving with potato salad.

Preheat an oven to 400°F (200°C).

In a frying pan over medium heat, melt the butter. Add the green onions and sauté, stirring, until soft, about 8 minutes. Add the mushrooms and continue to cook, stirring occasionally, until they release their liquid and it evaporates, about 5 minutes. Remove from the heat and let cool slightly.

Transfer the onion-mushroom mixture to a bowl and add the bread crumbs, pork, beef, egg, garlic, parsley, chicken stock, salt and the pepper to taste. Mix well. Pack into an 8½-by-4½-by-2½-inch (21.5-by-11.5-by-6-cm) loaf pan. Bake until an instant-read thermometer inserted into the center of the meat loaf reads 155°F (68°C), 45–50 minutes. Or test by cutting into the center; it should be cooked through.

Meanwhile, make the sauce: In a saucepan over medium-high heat, combine the ketchup or tomato sauce, sugar, water, vinegar, soy sauce and cayenne. Heat, stirring occasionally, until the mixture comes to a boil, then immediately whisk in the cornstarch-water mixture. Stir constantly until thickened, about 30 seconds. Remove from the heat and let cool to room temperature.

When the meat loaf is done, remove it from the oven, cover to keep warm, and let stand for 20 minutes before slicing. Pour off any excess fat in the pan. Cut the meat loaf into slices ½ inch (12 mm) thick. Serve immediately with the sweet-and-hot sauce on the side.

Serves 6

Scalloped Potatoes and Ham with Cheddar

2 cups (16 fl oz/500 ml) water
1½ lb (750 g) ham steak, cut ¼ inch (6 mm) thick, trimmed of excess fat and cut into 1–1½-inch (2.5–4-cm) dice
1 teaspoon vegetable oil
3½ lb (1.75 kg) baking potatoes, peeled and cut crosswise into slices ⅛ inch (3 mm) thick
6 tablespoons unsalted butter
6 tablespoons all-purpose (plain) flour
3 cups (24 fl oz/750 ml) warm milk
¾ lb (375 g) extra-sharp Cheddar cheese, shredded
1 tablespoon Dijon-style mustard
pinch of cayenne pepper
salt and freshly ground black pepper

This old-fashioned casserole is substantial enough to serve as a main course with just a green salad. Other cheeses, such as smoked Cheddar, can be substituted for the extra-sharp Cheddar. For blue-cheese lovers, substitute ¼ pound (125 g) blue cheese for the same amount of the Cheddar.

In a saucepan, bring the water to a boil. Add the ham and simmer for 30 seconds. Remove from the heat, drain well and discard the water. Set the ham aside.

Grease a 13-by-9-inch (33-by-23-cm) baking dish with the vegetable oil. Layer one-fourth of the potatoes on the bottom of the dish. Distribute one-third of the ham over the potatoes. Repeat the layers in the same manner until all of the potatoes and ham have been used. The top layer should be potatoes.

Preheat an oven to 350°F (180°C).

In a saucepan over medium heat, melt the butter. Add the flour and let the mixture bubble, stirring constantly, for 2 minutes. Gradually add the milk and cook, stirring, until the mixture thickens, 4–5 minutes longer. Remove from the heat and stir in the cheese, mustard, cayenne pepper and salt and pepper to taste. Return the pan to low heat and stir constantly just until the cheese melts, 1–2 minutes. Pour the cheese sauce evenly over the potatoes and ham.

Bake, uncovered, until the potatoes can be easily pierced with a skewer and are golden brown on top, about 1 hour.

Spoon the casserole onto warmed plates and serve at once.

Serves 6–8

Moroccan-Style Broiled Pork Chops

1½ teaspoons ground cumin

1½ teaspoons sweet paprika

½ teaspoon ground turmeric

¼ teaspoon cayenne pepper

3 cloves garlic

⅓ cup (2 oz/60 g) finely chopped
  yellow onion

salt and freshly ground pepper

6 tablespoons chopped fresh cilantro
  (fresh coriander), plus fresh cilantro
  sprigs for garnish

6 tablespoons chopped fresh parsley,
  preferably flat-leaf (Italian)

5 tablespoons fresh lemon juice

5 tablespoons extra-virgin olive oil

1 tablespoon water

6 center-cut pork chops, each about
  ½ lb (250 g) and 1–1½ inches
  (2.5–4 cm) thick, trimmed of
  excess fat

lemon wedges

The marinade for these pork chops is called chermoula, *and it is used in Moroccan cuisine to enhance the flavors of a variety of foods. Lamb chops can be used in place of the pork chops, and both can be marinated several hours before broiling. The chops can also be grilled over a charcoal fire, using the same timing. Serve with steamed couscous or rice.*

*I*n a blender or a food processor fitted with the metal blade, combine the cumin, paprika, turmeric, cayenne, garlic, onion, salt and pepper to taste, chopped cilantro, parsley, lemon juice, olive oil and water. Process until smooth. Place the pork chops in a single layer in a shallow, non-aluminum dish and pour the mixture over the top. Turn over the chops to coat them evenly on both sides with the marinade. Cover and refrigerate for 1 hour.

Preheat a broiler (griller).

Place the pork chops on the rack of a broiler pan. Brush any of the marinade remaining in the dish over the tops of the chops, distributing it evenly. Slip the pan under the broiler about 3 inches (7.5 cm) from the heat source and broil (grill), turning once, until the pork is golden on the outside, firm to the touch, and pale pink when cut in the center, about 10 minutes per side.

Transfer the chops to a warmed platter or plates and garnish with the lemon wedges and cilantro sprigs. Serve immediately.

Serves 6

Crown Roast of Pork with Sausage and Herb Stuffing

1 crown roast of pork with 16 chops,
  about 6 lb (3 kg)
salt and freshly ground pepper

FOR THE SAUSAGE AND HERB STUFFING:
¼ cup (2 oz/60 g) unsalted butter
1 large yellow onion, minced
1 large celery stalk, cut into ¼-inch
  (6-mm) dice
2 cloves garlic, minced
½ lb (250 g) bulk sweet pork sausage,
  crumbled
2½ cups (5 oz/155 g) fresh herbed
  bread crumbs (recipe on page 14)
1 egg, well beaten
about ¼ cup (2 fl oz/60 ml) chicken
  stock (recipe on page 14)
salt and freshly ground pepper

Two trimmed rib ends of a pork loin are tied together to make a crown roast. It is simple to prepare, as the butcher does the hard part.

*P*osition a rack in the middle of an oven and preheat to 400°F (200°C).

Set the pork on a rack in a roasting pan. Season to taste with salt and pepper. Roast, uncovered, on the middle rack for 30 minutes. Reduce the heat to 325°F (165°C) and, basting frequently with the pan juices, continue to roast for 45 minutes.

Meanwhile, make the stuffing: In a large frying pan over medium-low heat, melt the butter. Add the onion and celery and sauté, stirring occasionally, until very soft, about 15 minutes. Add the garlic and sausage and cook, stirring, until the sausage is browned, about 10 minutes longer. Using a slotted spoon, transfer the sausage mixture to a bowl. Discard the fat in the pan.

Add the bread crumbs and egg to the sausage mixture. Add enough of the chicken stock just to moisten the stuffing, then season to taste with salt and pepper. Mix well.

Mound the stuffing in the center of the crown roast and return the roast to the oven. Bake until an instant-read thermometer inserted into the center of the roast away from the bone registers 150°F (82°C) or a chop is pale pink when cut in the center, about 30 minutes longer. (Check periodically and cover the rib ends with foil if they brown before the meat is done).

Remove the roast from the oven, cover with a large piece of aluminum foil and let stand for 10 minutes before carving. To serve, cut the meat between the rib bones. Accompany each serving with a spoonful of stuffing.

Serves 6–8

Salad of Grilled Pork, Pears and Toasted Pecans

½ cup (2 oz/60 g) pecans
1 tablespoon peanut oil
salt and freshly ground pepper
pinch of sugar
2 pork tenderloins, about ¾ lb (375 g)
  each, trimmed of excess fat
1 tablespoon olive oil

FOR THE DRESSING:
6 tablespoons olive oil
2 tablespoons sherry vinegar
1 tablespoon hazelnut (filbert) oil
salt and freshly ground pepper

2 firm but ripe pears, preferably Bosc,
  halved and cored
3 large handfuls assorted greens, such
  as red leaf or butter lettuce and/or
  bitter greens such as frisée, radicchio,
  arugula (rocket) and mizuna
  (6–8 cups/6–8 oz/185–250 g),
  carefully washed and dried

Apples and walnuts can be substituted for the pears and pecans. The pork can also be cooked in a broiler (griller): Position the oiled pork tenderloins about 4 inches (10 cm) from the heat source and cook as directed for the charcoal grill. Accompany the salad with your favorite bread.

Prepare a fire in a charcoal grill. Preheat an oven to 350°F (180°C).

In a bowl, combine the pecans, peanut oil, salt and pepper to taste and sugar and toss well to coat the nuts. Spread the pecans on a baking sheet and bake until lightly golden, 5–7 minutes. Let cool.

Brush the pork tenderloins with the 1 tablespoon olive oil and season to taste with salt and pepper. Place on the grill rack 4 inches (10 cm) above the heat source and grill, turning occasionally to brown evenly, until firm to the touch and pale pink when cut in the thickest portion, about 12 minutes. Remove from the grill rack, cover with aluminum foil and let rest for 2–3 minutes before carving. Then cut crosswise into slices ¼ inch (6 mm) thick.

To make the dressing, in a small bowl, whisk together the olive oil, sherry vinegar, hazelnut oil, and salt and pepper to taste.

Cut the pears lengthwise into very thin slices. In a large bowl, combine the pear slices, greens, pork, pecans and dressing and toss to mix well. Transfer to a platter and serve immediately.

Serves 6

Pecan-Crusted Pork Chops

2 cups (8 oz/250 g) pecans
1 teaspoon salt
¼ teaspoon freshly ground pepper
½ cup (2½ oz/75 g) all-purpose
   (plain) flour
3 eggs
6 center-cut pork loin chops, each
   about 6 oz (185 g) and 1 inch
   (2.5 cm) thick, trimmed of excess fat
3 tablespoons unsalted butter
fresh parsley sprigs, preferably flat-leaf
   (Italian)

Any kind of nuts can be substituted for the pecans in this recipe. Try walnuts, hazelnuts (filberts), almonds or a combination. Serve with plum and ginger chutney or pear and mustard chutney (recipes on page 15).

Preheat an oven to 350°F (180°C). Spread the pecans on a baking sheet and bake until lightly golden, 5–7 minutes. Let cool and then chop finely. Place in a shallow bowl and add the salt and pepper. Stir to mix well. Raise the oven temperature to 375°F (190°C).

Place the flour in another shallow bowl. In a third bowl, whisk the eggs together until well blended.

Coating evenly and completely at each step, first dip the pork chops, one at a time, into the flour, shaking off any excess. Then dip the chops into the egg and then the finely chopped pecans.

In a large ovenproof frying pan over medium heat, melt the butter. Add the pork chops in a single layer and cook uncovered, turning once, until golden on both sides, 5–6 minutes total. Place the frying pan in the oven and continue to bake until firm to the touch and pale pink when cut in the center, 10–12 minutes; do not allow the nut coating to burn.

Transfer the pork chops to a warmed platter and garnish with the parsley sprigs. Serve immediately.

Serves 6

Southwest Pork Stir-fry

1 green bell pepper (capsicum)
1 yellow bell pepper (capsicum)
1 red bell pepper (capsicum)
4 tablespoons vegetable oil
1 large red (Spanish) onion, cut into small wedges
½–1 fresh jalapeño or serrano chili pepper, seeded and minced
2 pork tenderloins, about 1½ lb (750 g) total weight, trimmed of excess fat
½ cup (4 fl oz/125 ml) chicken stock *(recipe on page 14)*
1 tablespoon cornstarch (cornflour)
2 teaspoons ground cumin
3 cloves garlic, minced
15–20 red cherry tomatoes
salt and freshly ground pepper
4 tablespoons fresh cilantro (fresh coriander) leaves

This simple-to-prepare stir-fry draws upon the robust flavors of the American Southwest. If you like, add 1 cup (6 oz/185 g) steamed fresh corn kernels with the cherry tomatoes. Yellow cherry tomatoes can be substituted for half of the red ones. Enjoy this dish as a filling for tacos with melted Jack and Cheddar cheeses, or spoon it over a bowl of rice to serve as a main course.

Remove the stems, seeds and ribs from the bell peppers. Cut them lengthwise into strips ¼ inch (6 mm) wide.

In a wok or a large, deep frying pan over medium-high heat, warm 2 tablespoons of the vegetable oil. Add the onion, chili pepper and bell pepper strips and stir and toss until the peppers have softened but are still crisp, 6–8 minutes. Remove the pan from the heat and transfer the mixture to a bowl. Set the bowl and the pan aside.

Cut the pork tenderloins lengthwise into quarters, then cut them crosswise into pieces ¼ inch (6 mm) thick. In a large bowl, mix together the pork pieces, chicken stock, cornstarch, cumin and garlic. Return the pan used for cooking the onion-pepper mixture to the stove top over medium-high heat and add the remaining 2 tablespoons oil. Add the pork mixture and stir and toss until the pork is cooked, 3–4 minutes. Return the onion-pepper mixture to the pan, along with the cherry tomatoes and salt and pepper to taste. Stir and toss for 1 minute.

Transfer to a warmed platter and garnish with the cilantro leaves. Serve immediately.

Serves 6

Polenta with Pork Sausages and Tomatoes

8 cups (64 fl oz/2 l) water
1½ teaspoons salt, plus salt to taste
2½ cups (15 oz/470 g) polenta
3 tablespoons olive oil
1 yellow onion, minced
3 sweet pork sausages, about ¾ lb (375 g) total weight, pricked with a fork
3 spicy pork sausages, about ¾ lb (375 g) total weight, pricked with a fork
3 cups (18 oz/560 g) peeled, seeded and chopped tomatoes (fresh or canned)
freshly ground pepper
3 tablespoons unsalted butter
1 teaspoon chopped fresh rosemary
½ cup (2 oz/60 g) freshly grated Parmesan cheese

The coarsely ground Italian cornmeal known as polenta is used in a variety of dishes, both sweet and savory, in northern Italy. Sautéed red, green and yellow bell pepper (capsicum) can be added to this recipe. Garnish with grated pecorino cheese, if you prefer, and a few leaves of fresh flat-leaf (Italian) parsley.

*I*n a large saucepan over high heat, bring the water to a rolling boil. Add the 1½ teaspoons salt. Add the polenta in a slow, steady stream, whisking constantly. As soon as all of the polenta has been added, reduce the heat to low and switch to a wooden spoon. Cook, stirring often, until it is thick and the spoon stands upright, about 30 minutes.

Meanwhile, in a large frying pan or sauté pan over medium heat, warm the olive oil. Add the onion and sauté, stirring occasionally, until very soft, about 10 minutes. Add the sausages and cook, turning occasionally, until they are firm to the touch and cooked through, about 10 minutes.

Pour off any excess fat in the pan. Add the tomatoes and raise the heat to high. Cook, uncovered, until the tomato sauce thickens, about 10 minutes. Season to taste with salt and pepper.

When the polenta is done, stir in the butter, rosemary, and salt and pepper to taste. To serve, spoon the polenta onto a warmed serving platter or plates and make a well in the center. Cut the sausages in half on the diagonal and spoon the sausages and tomato sauce into the well. Sprinkle with the Parmesan cheese and serve immediately.

Serves 6

Pork Tenderloin Stuffed with Onion Marmalade

3 large pork tenderloins, about ¾–1 lb
   (375–500 g) each, trimmed of
   excess fat
1 tablespoon olive oil
3 cloves garlic, minced
¼ teaspoon cumin
¼ teaspoon cayenne pepper
¼ teaspoon ground cloves
salt and freshly ground black pepper

FOR THE ONION MARMALADE:
2 tablespoons olive oil
2 yellow onions, thinly sliced
1 teaspoon grated orange zest
¾ cup (6 fl oz/180 ml) fresh orange
   juice
⅓ cup (2 oz/60 g) golden raisins
   (sultanas)
¼ cup (2 fl oz/60 ml) sherry vinegar
   or white wine vinegar
2 teaspoons sugar
1 cup (8 fl oz/250 ml) water
salt and freshly ground pepper

½ cup (4 fl oz/125 ml) dry white wine
2 cups (16 fl oz/500 ml) chicken stock
   (recipe on page 14)
fresh flat-leaf (Italian) parsley leaves,
   optional

*B*utterfly the pork tenderloins by making a long slit down the length of each tenderloin, cutting just deep enough so that the tenderloin opens up to lay flat; do not to cut all the way through (see page 9). Flatten the tenderloins and pound gently with a meat pounder. Place in a single layer in a baking dish. In a bowl, combine the olive oil, minced garlic, cumin, cayenne, cloves, and salt and black pepper to taste. Rub the pork with the mixture, cover and refrigerate for 1 hour or as long as overnight.

To make the onion marmalade, in a frying pan over medium heat, warm the oil. Add the onions and sauté, stirring occasionally, until lightly golden, about 15 minutes. Add the orange zest, orange juice, raisins, vinegar, sugar, water, and salt and pepper to taste. Cover and cook over low heat until the onions are very soft, about 30 minutes. Uncover, raise the heat to medium-high and cook until the onions are dry, about 10 minutes.

Lay the pork tenderloins, cut side up, on a work surface. Spread the onion mixture over the pork, distributing it evenly. Close up the tenderloins and, using kitchen string, tie at 1-inch (2.5-cm) intervals.

Place the pork in a heavy-bottomed pot and add the wine and stock. Cover, bring to a boil, reduce the heat to very low and simmer until the pork is firm to the touch and pale pink when cut in the thickest portion, about 30 minutes. Transfer the pork to a cutting board; keep warm. Raise the heat to high and, stirring occasionally, reduce the broth by half, about 10 minutes. Strain the broth and keep warm.

Snip the strings on the tenderloins. Cut crosswise into slices ½ inch (12 mm) thick. Arrange on a warmed platter and spoon the broth on top. Garnish with parsley, if desired, and serve.

Serves 6

Fillet of Lamb with Roasted Peppers and Onions

¼ cup (2 fl oz/60 ml) olive oil

1 tablespoon minced fresh rosemary

salt and freshly ground pepper

3 racks of lamb, 1½–2 lb (750 g–1 kg) each, boned and trimmed of fat

2 red bell peppers (capsicums), quartered lengthwise, seeded and deribbed

2 yellow bell peppers (capsicums), quartered lengthwise, seeded and deribbed

3 large red (Spanish) onions, cut into slices ¾ inch (2 cm) thick

FOR THE HERB DRESSING:

¼ cup (2 fl oz/60 ml) extra-virgin olive oil

1 tablespoon red wine vinegar

2 teaspoons minced mixed fresh herbs, such as rosemary, oregano, mint, chives and thyme, in any combination

salt and freshly ground pepper

fresh rosemary sprigs for garnish

To make this recipe, the fillet must first be removed from each lamb rack. You can bone the rack yourself by carefully cutting around the fillet with a long, sharp boning knife, or ask your butcher to do it.

In a bowl, whisk together the olive oil, rosemary and a pinch each of salt and pepper. Add the lamb fillets and turn to coat completely. Marinate for 1 hour at room temperature.

Meanwhile, prepare a fire in a charcoal grill.

When the lamb has marinated for 1 hour, add the bell peppers and coat them completely with the marinade. Arrange the onion slices on a plate and brush them with any marinade remaining in the bottom of the bowl.

To make the dressing, in a bowl whisk together the olive oil, vinegar and mixed herbs. Season to taste with salt and pepper. Set aside.

Place the lamb fillets on the grill rack about 4 inches (10 cm) from the heat source. Grill, turning the lamb every 5 minutes, until it is well browned on the outside and pink when cut in the thickest portion, 20–25 minutes total. When the lamb has been on the grill 10 minutes, place the onion slices on the grill and cook them until they soften on one side, 5–7 minutes. Carefully turn over the onions and, at the same time, place the bell peppers, skin side down, on the grill rack. Continue to cook the onions and peppers, turning the peppers once, until they are soft, 5–10 minutes longer.

When the lamb and vegetables are cooked, transfer them to a warmed platter. Quickly whisk the dressing and drizzle it evenly over the top. Garnish with the rosemary sprigs and serve at once.

Serves 6

Grilled Lamb Burgers with Mint, Tomatoes and Garlic

2 lb (1 kg) ground (minced) lamb
¼ cup (1½ oz/45 g) minced red (Spanish) onion
2 cloves garlic, minced
6 tablespoons chopped fresh mint, plus fresh mint sprigs for garnish
½ teaspoon ground cumin
1 teaspoon salt, plus salt to taste
½ teaspoon coarsely ground pepper, plus coarsely ground pepper to taste
24 whole cloves garlic
4 tablespoons extra-virgin olive oil
4 tomatoes, peeled, seeded and chopped
6 slices rustic country-style bread

This is a terrific dish for lamb and garlic lovers. Serve it during the summer when the tomatoes and mint are at their best and the temperatures are perfect for outdoor grilling.

*I*n a bowl, combine the lamb, onion, minced garlic, 2 tablespoons of the chopped mint, cumin, the 1 teaspoon salt and the ½ teaspoon pepper. Mix well and form into 6 patties each about ½ inch (12 mm) thick. Cover and refrigerate for 1 hour.

Prepare a fire in a charcoal grill.

Bring a small saucepan three-fourths full of water to a boil. Add the garlic cloves and simmer, uncovered, until just soft, 10–15 minutes. Drain and reserve the garlic.

In a frying pan or sauté pan over medium heat, warm 2 tablespoons of the olive oil. Add the tomatoes, the remaining 4 tablespoons chopped mint, the garlic cloves and salt and pepper to taste. Simmer until the juices evaporate and the sauce thickens slightly, 5–10 minutes. Remove from the heat, cover and keep warm.

Brush the bread slices with the remaining 2 tablespoons olive oil and place on the grill rack. Grill, turning once, until golden, about 5 minutes on each side. Grill the lamb burgers at the same time, turning them once, until medium-rare and pink when cut in the thickest portion, 4–5 minutes on each side.

To serve, place 1 slice of grilled bread on each plate and top with a lamb burger. Spoon the warm sauce on top and garnish with the mint sprigs. Serve immediately.

Serves 6

Greek Lamb Baked with Yogurt and Herb Sauce

FOR THE YOGURT AND HERB SAUCE:
2 cups (1 lb/500 g) plain yogurt
½ cucumber, peeled, halved
  lengthwise and seeded
salt
4 cloves garlic, minced
1 tablespoon chopped fresh mint
2 teaspoons chopped fresh dill
1 tablespoon extra-virgin olive oil
1 tablespoon fresh lemon juice

FOR THE LAMB:
8 cloves garlic, thinly sliced
3 bay leaves, ground to a powder
  in a mortar or in a spice grinder
½ teaspoon ground cinnamon
1½ teaspoons dried oregano
salt and freshly ground pepper
1 leg of lamb, 5–6 lb (2.5–3 kg),
  trimmed of excess fat and boned
  (see page 11)
2 tablespoons extra-virgin olive oil

To begin making the yogurt and herb sauce, line a sieve with cheesecloth (muslin) and place over a bowl. Add the yogurt, then place in the refrigerator and let drain for 4 hours.

To prepare the lamb, in a small bowl, combine the sliced garlic, bay leaf powder, cinnamon, oregano, and salt and pepper to taste and mix well. Lay the lamb flat, with the outside surface facing down. Using a sharp knife, make incisions 1 inch (2.5 cm) deep all over the inside surface of the lamb. Insert the garlic mixture into the slits. Roll up into a bundle and, using kitchen string, tie as you would a gift. Rub with the 2 tablespoons olive oil and salt and pepper to taste. Wrap tightly in a double layer of aluminum foil.

Preheat an oven to 200°F (93°C). Place the lamb on a rack in a roasting pan. Pour water into the pan to just below the rack. Bake until an instant-read thermometer inserted into the thickest portion of meat registers 130°–135°F (54°–57°C) for medium-rare or the meat is pink when cut with a sharp knife, about 4 hours. Add water as needed to maintain the original level.

Meanwhile, finish making the sauce: Shred the cucumber on the large holes of a shredder to measure 1 cup (5 oz/155 g). Place on paper towels and sprinkle with salt. Let drain for 30 minutes.

In a bowl, combine the drained yogurt, cucumber, minced garlic, mint, dill and the 1 tablespoon olive oil. Mix well. Stir in the lemon juice and salt to taste. Set aside.

When the lamb is ready, unwrap the foil, reserving any juices, and transfer the meat to a cutting board. Cover with aluminum foil and let rest for 10 minutes, then snip off the string. Cut across the grain into thin slices; arrange on a warmed platter. Drizzle any juices in the foil package over the top. Serve the yogurt sauce on the side.

Serves 6

Broiled Lamb Chops with Coriander-Orange Butter

Broiled lamb chops are classic French bistro fare. Oven-roasted potatoes are the ideal Gallic accompaniment.

FOR THE CORIANDER-ORANGE BUTTER:

6 tablespoons unsalted butter, at room temperature

3 tablespoons chopped fresh cilantro (fresh coriander)

½ teaspoon ground coriander

¾ teaspoon grated orange zest

salt and freshly ground pepper

12 lamb chops, about 3 lb (1.5 kg) total weight, each 1 inch (2.5 cm) thick, trimmed of excess fat

2 tablespoons olive oil

salt and freshly ground pepper

fresh cilantro (fresh coriander) sprigs

orange wedges

To make the butter, in a small bowl and using a fork, mash together the butter, chopped cilantro, ground coriander, orange zest, and salt and pepper to taste. Cover and refrigerate for 15 minutes.

Remove the butter from the refrigerator. Place a piece of plastic wrap 10 inches (25 cm) square on a work surface. Using a rubber spatula, mound the butter along the center of the plastic wrap. Drape one side of the plastic wrap over the butter and then roll the butter into a tube shape about 1 inch (2.5 cm) in diameter and 3 inches (7.5 cm) long. Twist the ends of the plastic wrap in opposite directions, like a candy wrapper, and refrigerate the butter until firm.

Preheat a broiler (griller).

Brush the lamb chops on both sides with the olive oil and season to taste with salt and pepper. Place on a broiler pan. Slip the pan under the broiler about 4 inches (10 cm) from the heat source. Broil (grill) until browned on the first side, about 5 minutes. Turn over the lamb chops and continue to broil until browned on the second side and pink when cut in the center, about 5 minutes longer.

Remove from the broiler and place 2 lamb chops on each plate. Remove the butter from the refrigerator and remove the plastic wrap. Cut the butter into slices ¼ inch (6 mm) thick. Place 1 slice on top of each lamb chop. Garnish with the cilantro sprigs and orange wedges and serve immediately.

Serves 6

Lamb Sandwich with Feta and Cucumber Salad

FOR THE FETA AND CUCUMBER SALAD:

6 oz (185 g) feta cheese

2 tablespoons extra-virgin olive oil

2 tablespoons fresh lemon juice

salt and freshly ground pepper

1 cucumber, peeled, halved lengthwise,
    seeded and cut into ½-inch (12-mm)
    dice

½ small red (Spanish) onion, cut into
    ¼-inch (6-mm) dice

1 tablespoon chopped fresh mint

1 tablespoon chopped fresh parsley,
    preferably flat-leaf (Italian)

1 tablespoon chopped fresh dill

1 piece boneless leg of lamb, 1½–2 lb
    (750 g–1 kg), trimmed of excess fat
    and butterflied (see page 11)

1 tablespoon extra-virgin olive oil

6 pita breads, each 6 inches (15 cm)
    in diameter, cut into halves

For added color and flavor, tuck a few tomato slices, lettuce leaves or pitted Kalamata olives into this delicious sandwich. Inspired by an Egyptian recipe, the salad is also good spread on wedges of toasted bread or pita triangles and served as a first course.

Prepare a fire in a charcoal grill or preheat a broiler (griller).

To make the salad, crumble the feta into a bowl and add the olive oil, lemon juice, and salt and pepper to taste. Using a fork, mash together to mix thoroughly. Stir in the cucumber, onion, mint, parsley and dill. Set aside.

Brush the lamb with the 1 tablespoon olive oil. Place on a grill rack or broiler pan. Grill or broil 4 inches (10 cm) from the heat source until golden brown on the first side, about 15 minutes. Turn over the lamb and continue to cook until golden brown on the second side and an instant-read thermometer inserted into the thickest portion registers 130°–135°F (54°–57°C) for medium-rare or the meat is slightly pink when cut with a sharp knife, about 15 minutes longer. Transfer the lamb to a cutting board, cover with aluminum foil and let rest for 10 minutes before carving.

Just before the lamb is cooked, preheat an oven to 350°F (180°C). Wrap the pita halves in aluminum foil, place in the oven and heat until warm, about 10 minutes.

Slice the meat across the grain on the diagonal. Season to taste with salt and pepper. Open the pita pockets and evenly distribute the lamb and feta and cucumber salad among the halves. Place 2 half sandwiches on each plate and serve immediately.

Serves 6

Lamb and Lentil Soup

1½ lb (750 g) boneless lamb meat, trimmed of excess fat and cut into small cubes

2 tablespoons olive oil

½ teaspoon ground cumin

½ teaspoon sweet paprika

2 bay leaves

1 piece lemon peel, about ½ inch (12 mm) wide and 2 inches (5 cm) long

⅛–¼ teaspoon crushed red pepper flakes

8 cups (64 fl oz/2 l) water

1¼ cups (9 oz/280 g) dried lentils

1 yellow onion, cut into ½-inch (12-mm) dice

1 large carrot, peeled and cut into ½-inch (12-mm) dice

¾ cup (¾ oz/20 g) chopped fresh cilantro (fresh coriander)

salt and freshly ground pepper

This soup is so thick it is almost a stew. It can be made up to 3 days in advance and simply reheated for serving. Dried beans such as chick-peas (garbanzo beans), small white (navy) beans, pinto beans or black beans can be substituted for the lentils. If you are using any of these dried beans, soak them for a few hours in plenty of cold water to cover, then drain and simmer in fresh water to cover until their skins begin to crack and the beans are tender. Cooking times will vary depending upon the type of bean used.

*I*n a soup pot, combine the lamb, olive oil, cumin, paprika, bay leaves, lemon peel, red pepper flakes and 2 cups (16 fl oz/500 ml) of the water. Bring to a boil, reduce the heat to low, cover and simmer gently until the lamb is tender, 1½–2 hours.

Add the remaining 6 cups (48 fl oz/1.5 l) water, the lentils, onion and carrot and simmer, uncovered, over low heat until the lentils are just tender, 20–30 minutes.

Discard the bay leaves and lemon peel. Stir in the cilantro and salt and pepper to taste. Ladle into warmed bowls and serve immediately.

Serves 6

Roast Leg of Lamb with Vegetables

6 cloves garlic, thinly sliced

1 tablespoon chopped fresh mint, plus fresh mint sprigs for garnish

½ teaspoon chopped fresh rosemary

salt and freshly ground pepper

1 leg of lamb, 5–6 lb (2.5–3 kg), trimmed of excess fat

2 tablespoons olive oil

2½–3 lb (1.25–1.5 kg) small red potatoes, unpeeled and well scrubbed

8 carrots, peeled, cut into 2-inch (5-cm) lengths, boiled in water for 5 minutes and drained

When properly cooked, a simple roast leg of lamb is one of the most delicious dishes you can prepare.

In a small bowl, mix together the garlic, chopped mint, rosemary, and salt and pepper to taste. Using a sharp paring knife, make incisions 1 inch (2.5 cm) deep all over the meat surface and insert the garlic mixture into the slits. Rub the meat evenly with the olive oil.

Position a rack in the bottom of an oven and preheat to 450°F (230°C).

Place the lamb on a rack in a large roasting pan. Season with salt and pepper. Roast the lamb for 15 minutes. Add the potatoes and carrots to the pan and roast 15 minutes longer. Turn the lamb over and reduce the heat to 325°F (165°C). Continue to roast until an instant-read thermometer inserted into the thickest portion away from the bone registers 130°–135°F (54°–57°C) or the meat is pink when cut with a sharp knife, about 45 minutes.

When the meat is done, transfer it to a cutting board, cover with aluminum foil and let rest for 10 minutes before carving. Pierce the potatoes and carrots. If they are tender, remove them from the oven as well. If not, leave them in the oven while the lamb is resting.

To serve, cut the lamb across the grain into thin slices (or leave it whole to slice at the table) and arrange on a warmed platter with the potatoes and carrots. Garnish with mint sprigs and serve immediately.

Serves 6–8

Penne with Lamb, Zucchini, Tomatoes and Basil

2 tablespoons extra-virgin olive oil
1 small yellow onion, cut into 8 wedges
2 cloves garlic, minced
¾ lb (375 g) small zucchini (courgettes), cut into pieces ½ inch (12 mm) thick on the sharp diagonal and then cut each piece in half lengthwise to make sticks
1 lb (500 g) ground (minced) lean lamb
salt
¾ lb (375 g) dried penne pasta
4 large tomatoes, chopped
½ cup (4 fl oz/125 ml) chicken stock (recipe on page 14)
freshly ground pepper
½ cup (½ oz/15 g) fresh basil leaves, cut into thin strips
½ cup (2 oz/60 g) freshly grated Parmesan cheese

Other pasta shapes such as bowties, rigatoni, fettuccine or linguine go well with this sauce. Serve with red wine and plenty of crusty Italian bread.

*B*ring a large pot three-fourths full of water to a boil.

Meanwhile, in a large frying pan or sauté pan over medium heat, warm the olive oil. Add the onion and sauté, stirring, until soft, about 10 minutes. Add the garlic and continue to sauté, stirring, for 2 minutes. Add the zucchini sticks and cook, stirring occasionally, until they begin to soften, about 5 minutes.

Crumble the lamb into the pan and cook, stirring occasionally, until the lamb loses its pinkness, about 5 minutes. Remove the pan from the heat and pour off the fat. Meanwhile, add salt to taste to the boiling water and then add the pasta. Cook until just tender, about 15 minutes or according to package directions.

Return the lamb to medium-high heat. Add the tomatoes, chicken stock, and salt and pepper to taste. Cook until the lamb and zucchini are cooked through, about 5 minutes.

When the pasta is ready, drain and place in a large warmed serving bowl. Add the lamb sauce, basil and Parmesan cheese and toss well. Serve immediately.

Serves 6

Lamb and Eggplant Brochettes with Provençal Dressing

1½ lb (750 g) boneless leg of lamb,
  trimmed of excess fat and cut into
  1–1½-inch (2.5–4-cm) cubes
8 slender (Asian) eggplants
  (aubergines), unpeeled, cut into
  1-inch (2.5-cm) pieces
3 tablespoons pure olive oil
salt and freshly ground pepper

FOR THE PROVENÇAL DRESSING:
6 tablespoons extra-virgin olive oil
2 tablespoons red wine vinegar
1 tablespoon tomato paste
1 clove garlic, minced
¼ teaspoon chopped fresh rosemary
¼ teaspoon chopped fresh thyme
¼ teaspoon chopped fresh oregano
salt and freshly ground pepper

When making lamb brochettes, use a good cut, such as leg, or the meat may be tough. Other vegetables can be used in place of or in addition to the eggplant—zucchini (courgettes); red, yellow or green bell pepper (capsicum) chunks; yellow or red cherry tomatoes; or blanched pearl onions. Steamed couscous or rice makes a good accompaniment. Garnish the dish with sprigs of thyme or oregano, if you like.

Soak 12 bamboo skewers in water to cover for 30 minutes. Meanwhile, place the lamb and eggplants in a bowl. Add the pure olive oil and salt and pepper to taste and toss well. Let stand at room temperature until ready to cook.

To make the dressing, in a small bowl, whisk together the extra-virgin olive oil, vinegar, tomato paste, garlic, rosemary, thyme, oregano, and salt and pepper to taste. Set aside.

Prepare a fire in a charcoal grill or preheat a broiler (griller).

Drain the skewers. Thread equal amounts of lamb and eggplant onto each skewer, alternating the lamb and eggplant pieces. Place the skewers on the grill rack or on a broiler pan 4 inches (10 cm) from the heat source and grill or broil, turning occasionally, until the lamb is still pink inside and the eggplant is golden and cooked through, 10–12 minutes total.

Transfer the skewers to a warmed platter. Quickly whisk the dressing and drizzle it over the skewers. Serve at once.

Serves 6

Grilled Butterflied Leg of Lamb with Mint Mustard

¼ cup (2 fl oz/60 ml) olive oil
3 cloves garlic, minced
salt and freshly ground pepper
1 leg of lamb, 5–6 lb (2.5–3 kg),
   trimmed of excess fat, boned and
   butterflied (*see page 11*)

FOR THE MINT MUSTARD:
6 tablespoons chopped fresh mint, plus
   fresh mint sprigs for garnish (optional)
3 tablespoons mayonnaise
¾ cup (6 oz/185 g) Dijon-style mustard
1 clove garlic, minced
1 teaspoon fresh lemon juice

Grilled butterflied leg of lamb can be served with a variety of other sauces. Try mint jelly, fruit chutney (recipes on page 15) or yogurt and herb sauce (recipe on page 67).

In a bowl, whisk together the olive oil, garlic, and salt and pepper to taste. Place the lamb in a shallow dish and rub the mixture over the entire surface of the meat. Let stand at room temperature for 1 hour, or cover and refrigerate overnight.

Prepare a fire in a charcoal grill or preheat a broiler (griller).

To make the mint mustard, in a small bowl, stir together the chopped mint, mayonnaise, mustard, garlic and lemon juice. Set aside.

Place the lamb on the grill rack or in a broiler pan. Grill or broil 4 inches (10 cm) from the heat source until the first side is golden, about 15 minutes. Turn over the lamb and continue to cook until golden on the second side and an instant-read thermometer inserted into the thickest portion registers 130°–135°F (54°–57°C) for medium-rare or the meat is pink when cut with a sharp knife, about 15 minutes longer. Transfer to a cutting board and cover with aluminum foil. Let rest for 10 minutes before carving.

Cut the lamb across the grain into thin slices and arrange on a warmed platter. Garnish with the mint sprigs, if using, and serve the mint mustard alongside. Serve immediately.

Serves 6–8

Braised Lamb Shanks with White Beans

1½ cups (10½ oz/330 g) dried white
  kidney beans or cannellini beans
3 tablespoons olive oil
6 lamb shanks, ½–¾ lb (250–375 g)
  each
2 red (Spanish) onions, cut into ½-inch
  (12-mm) dice
2 large carrots, peeled and cut into
  ½-inch (12-mm) dice
6 cloves garlic, minced
1½ cups (12 fl oz/375 ml) dry red wine
1½ cups (12 fl oz/375 ml) chicken
  stock (recipe on page 14)
3 tablespoons tomato paste
1 cup (6 oz/185 g) peeled, seeded and
  chopped tomatoes (fresh or canned)
1 teaspoon chopped fresh thyme
1 bay leaf
salt and freshly ground pepper
1 tablespoon grated lemon zest
2 tablespoons chopped fresh parsley

This dish is a modern adaptation of ossobuco, *the classic northern Italian specialty of braised veal shanks. Here, it is served with white beans instead of the more traditional risotto. The lemon-and-parsley garnish is called* gremolata. *Feel free to use orange zest in place of the lemon zest, and oregano or thyme for the parsley.*

Pick over the beans and discard any stones; rinse well. Place in a bowl and add water to cover. Soak for at least 4 hours or as long as overnight.

Drain the beans and place in a saucepan with water to cover by 2 inches (5 cm). Bring to a boil, reduce the heat to low and simmer, uncovered, until the skins begin to crack and the beans are tender, 45–60 minutes. Drain the beans and set aside.

Meanwhile, in a deep, heavy pot over medium heat, warm the olive oil. Add the lamb shanks and brown on all sides, 10–12 minutes. Remove from the pan and set aside. Add the onions and carrots and sauté, stirring occasionally, until the onions are soft, about 10 minutes. Add the garlic and sauté, stirring, for 1 minute. Add the red wine, chicken stock, tomato paste, tomatoes, thyme and bay leaf and stir well. Return the lamb shanks to the pot. Raise the heat to high and bring to a boil. Reduce the heat to low, cover and simmer until the shanks can be easily pierced with a skewer, 1½–2 hours.

Add the beans, stir well, cover and simmer gently over low heat until the lamb begins to fall off the bones, about 30 minutes. Season to taste with salt and pepper.

In a small bowl, stir together the lemon zest and parsley. Transfer the lamb and beans to warmed plates and garnish with the lemon-parsley mixture. Serve immediately.

Serves 6

Moussaka

2 large globe eggplants (aubergines),
   1 lb (500 g) each, unpeeled, cut
   crosswise into slices ¼ inch
   (6 mm) thick
salt
7 tablespoons olive oil
1 large yellow onion, chopped
4 cloves garlic, minced
2 lb (1 kg) ground (minced) lamb,
   crumbled
2 cups (12 oz/375 g) peeled, seeded and
   chopped tomatoes (fresh or canned)
½ cup (4 fl oz/125 ml) dry white wine
1 teaspoon chopped fresh oregano
¼ teaspoon ground cinnamon
freshly ground pepper
3 tablespoons unsalted butter
¼ cup (1½ oz/45 g) all-purpose
   (plain) flour
2 cups (16 fl oz/500 ml) milk
⅛ teaspoon freshly ground nutmeg
6 tablespoons freshly grated Parmesan
   cheese
1 egg, lightly beaten

Preheat an oven to 400°F (200°C).

Lightly sprinkle the eggplant slices on both sides with salt, place in a colander and let stand for 30 minutes. Rinse the eggplant slices with cold water and blot dry with paper towels.

Oil 2 baking sheets with 1 tablespoon of the olive oil and place the eggplant slices in a single layer on the baking sheets. Brush the tops of the slices with 3 tablespoons of the oil. Bake until golden, turning occasionally, 10–15 minutes. Remove from the oven; let cool. Reduce the oven temperature to 350°F (180°C).

In a frying pan over medium heat, warm 2 tablespoons of the oil. Add the onion and sauté until very soft, about 10 minutes. Add the garlic and sauté for 1 minute. Raise the heat to high, add the lamb and cook, stirring often, until browned, about 5 minutes. Add the tomatoes, wine, oregano, cinnamon, and salt and pepper to taste. Bring to a boil, reduce the heat to low, cover and simmer until very thick, 30–40 minutes.

In a saucepan over medium heat, melt the butter. Add the flour and whisk constantly for 2 minutes. Gradually whisk in the milk, then bring to a boil, stirring constantly. Reduce the heat to low and simmer, stirring occasionally, until thickened, about 1 minute. Remove from the heat. Add the nutmeg, 1 tablespoon of the Parmesan cheese, and salt and pepper to taste.

Oil a 13-by-9-inch (33-by-23-cm) baking dish with the remaining 1 tablespoon oil. Place one-third of the eggplant slices in a single layer on the bottom. Then spread with half of the lamb sauce. Top with half of the remaining eggplant, then the remaining lamb sauce and finish with a layer of the remaining eggplant. Whisk the egg into the cream sauce and spread evenly on top. Sprinkle with the remaining 5 tablespoons cheese.

Bake until the top is golden, 50–60 minutes. Let cool slightly before cutting, then cut into individual portions.

Serves 6–8

Stir-fried Lamb Salad with Sesame-Lemon Dressing

4 tablespoons peanut oil

1 tablespoon Asian sesame oil

2 tablespoons dark soy sauce

2 tablespoons fresh lemon juice

2 tablespoons rice wine vinegar

salt and freshly ground pepper

1 large red (Spanish) onion, cut into small wedges

1 fresh jalapeño chili pepper, seeded and minced

4 cloves garlic, minced

2½ lb (1.25 kg) leg of lamb, trimmed of excess fat, boned (*see page 11*), then cut into thin strips 1½ inches (4 cm) long, ½ inch (12 mm) wide and ¼ inch (6 mm) thick

1 large head romaine (cos) lettuce, leaves carefully washed and dried and then cut crosswise into strips 1 inch (2.5 cm) wide

1 head radicchio, leaves separated, then cut crosswise into strips ½ inch (12 mm) wide

lemon wedges

If you like, garnish this dish with toasted sesame seeds, green (spring) onions or fresh cilantro (fresh coriander) sprigs. This salad makes a nice light luncheon main course or a great first course for a Chinese dinner.

In a small bowl, whisk together 2 tablespoons of the peanut oil, the sesame oil, soy sauce, lemon juice, rice wine vinegar, and salt and pepper to taste to make a dressing. Set aside.

In a large, deep frying pan or a wok over medium-high heat, warm the remaining 2 tablespoons peanut oil. Add the onion and stir and toss until it begins to soften, about 7 minutes. Add the chili pepper and garlic and stir and toss until the garlic is soft, about 1 minute.

Raise the heat to high, add the lamb and continue to stir and toss until the lamb is cooked, about 3 minutes. Season to taste with salt and pepper.

Transfer to a large bowl and add the romaine lettuce, radicchio and the reserved dressing. Toss gently to mix well. Place on a warmed platter and garnish with the lemon wedges. Serve immediately.

Serves 6

Sweet-and-Spicy Lamb Curry

2–2½ lb (1–1.25 kg) lamb stew meat, cut from the leg or shoulder, trimmed of excess fat and cut into 1-inch (2.5-cm) pieces
3 tablespoons all-purpose (plain) flour
3 tablespoons unsalted butter
2 yellow onions, chopped
1 celery stalk, cut into small dice
1 fresh jalapeño or serrano chili pepper, minced
4 cloves garlic, minced
2 cups (16 fl oz/500 ml) chicken stock (recipe on page 14)
3 tablespoons curry powder
1½ tablespoons peeled and grated fresh ginger
2½ cups (20 fl oz/625 ml) water
½ teaspoon salt, plus salt to taste
1 cup (7 oz/220 g) basmati rice, rinsed and drained
½ cup (4 fl oz/125 ml) golden raisins (sultanas), soaked in very hot water to cover for 30 minutes
2 firm green apples, such as Granny Smith or pippin, peeled, halved, cored and cut into small dice
¼ cup (2 fl oz/60 ml) coconut milk or heavy (double) cream
freshly ground pepper

Garnish this highly aromatic dish with toasted coconut, sliced bananas, toasted almonds or peanuts, dried currants, chopped green (spring) onions and/or fruit chutney (recipes on page 15).

*I*n a bowl, toss the lamb pieces with the flour to coat evenly. In a large, heavy pot over medium-high heat, melt the butter. Working in batches if necessary, add the lamb and brown on all sides, about 10 minutes; do not crowd the pot. Using a slotted spoon, transfer the lamb to a plate.

Reduce the heat to medium and add the onions, celery and chili pepper. Sauté, stirring occasionally, until the onions and celery are soft, about 10 minutes. Add the garlic and sauté, stirring, for 2 minutes. Return the lamb to the pot and add the chicken stock, curry powder and ginger. Stir well, cover and simmer over low heat until the meat is tender, 1½–2 hours.

About 20 minutes before the curry is done, in a heavy saucepan over high heat, bring the water and the ½ teaspoon salt to a boil. Add the rice, reduce the heat to low, cover and cook for 20 minutes; do not remove the cover. After 20 minutes, uncover the rice; the water should be absorbed and the rice should be tender. If the rice is not ready, re-cover and cook for 2–3 minutes longer until the rice is done. Remove from the heat, fluff the grains with a fork and keep warm.

While the rice is cooking, drain the raisins and add them to the curry, along with the apples and coconut milk or cream. Simmer, uncovered, over low heat until the sauce thickens, about 15 minutes. Season to taste with salt and pepper.

Mound the rice on a serving platter. Make a well in the center and spoon the curried lamb into the well. Serve immediately.

Serves 6

Lamb Stew with Artichokes

6 medium artichokes

juice of 1 lemon

4 tablespoons olive oil

2 yellow onions, coarsely chopped

1–2 tablespoons all-purpose (plain) flour

salt and freshly ground pepper

2½–3 lb (1.25–1.5 kg) lamb stew meat, cut into 2-inch (5-cm) chunks

1 bay leaf

½ teaspoon chopped fresh thyme

6 fresh parsley sprigs, preferably flat-leaf (Italian), plus fresh parsley leaves for garnish

½ teaspoon chopped fresh rosemary

3 cloves garlic, minced

1 cup (8 fl oz/250 ml) dry white wine

2 large tomatoes, peeled, seeded and coarsely chopped

1–2 cups (8–16 fl oz/250–500 ml) chicken stock (recipe on page 14)

Cut off the top half of each artichoke, then remove the tough outer leaves until only light green leaves remain. As the artichokes are trimmed, immerse them in a bowl of water to which the lemon juice has been added. Quarter each trimmed artichoke and scrape away the thistle. When all are quartered, drain and blot dry. In a frying pan over low heat, warm 2 tablespoons of the oil. Add the artichokes and cook, stirring occasionally, until tender, 20–30 minutes. Set aside.

Meanwhile, in a large soup pot over medium heat, warm the remaining 2 tablespoons oil. Add the onions and sauté until golden, about 15 minutes. Using a slotted spoon, transfer to a bowl.

Combine the flour and salt and pepper to taste in a bowl. Add the lamb chunks and toss to coat. Working in batches, add the lamb to the pot over medium-high heat and brown on all sides, 10–12 minutes.

Place the bay leaf, thyme and parsley sprigs on a square of cheesecloth (muslin), bring the corners together and tie securely with kitchen string to form a bouquet garni. When the lamb is browned, return the onions to the pan, along with the rosemary, garlic and the bouquet garni. Raise the heat to high and add the wine, scraping up any browned bits on the pan bottom. Add the tomatoes and enough stock to cover the meat. Bring to a boil, reduce the heat to low, cover and simmer until the meat is easily pierced with a skewer, about 1½ hours.

Using a slotted spoon, transfer the lamb to a bowl. Pour the broth through a fine-mesh sieve into a clean container; skim off the fat on the surface. Return the broth to the pot and bring to a simmer over medium-low heat. Simmer until slightly thickened, 5–10 minutes. Return the lamb to the pot and add the artichokes and salt and pepper to taste. Simmer for 2 minutes. Ladle into warmed bowls and garnish with the parsley leaves.

Serves 6

Stuffed Leg of Lamb

3 cloves garlic, finely chopped

¼ cup (2 oz/60 g) drained, oil-packed sun-dried tomatoes, thinly sliced

2 tablespoons pitted cured black olives, chopped

5 tablespoons chopped fresh parsley

1½ teaspoons chopped fresh rosemary

½ teaspoon chopped fresh sage, optional

1 cup (4 oz/125 g) dried herbed bread crumbs *(recipe on page 14)*

¼ cup (2 oz/60 g) unsalted butter, melted

salt and freshly ground pepper

1 leg of lamb, 5–6 lb (2.5–3 kg), trimmed of excess fat and boned *(see page 11)*

1 tablespoon olive oil

fresh rosemary and/or thyme sprigs

This recipe is a natural with steamed spinach and creamy mashed potatoes flavored with roasted garlic.

In a bowl, combine the garlic, sun-dried tomatoes, olives, parsley, chopped rosemary, sage (if using), bread crumbs, melted butter, and salt and pepper to taste. Mix well.

Lay the lamb flat on a work surface, with the outside surface facing down. Season with salt and pepper. Spread the crumb mixture evenly over the lamb. Roll up the lamb into a bundle roughly resembling its original shape, completely enclosing the stuffing. Using kitchen string, tie the roast as you would a gift. Season the outside with salt and pepper.

Position a rack in the bottom of an oven and preheat to 450°F (230°C).

In a large frying pan or sauté pan over medium heat, warm the olive oil. Add the lamb and brown on all sides, about 10 minutes.

Transfer the lamb to a rack in a roasting pan. Roast on the bottom oven rack for 30 minutes. Turn the lamb over and reduce the heat to 325°F (165°C). Continue to roast until an instant-read thermometer inserted into the thickest portion registers 130°–135°F (54°–57°C) or the meat is pink when cut with a sharp knife, about 45 minutes. Transfer to a cutting board, cover with aluminum foil and let rest for 10 minutes before carving.

To serve, snip off the string and discard. Cut the lamb across the grain into thin slices and arrange on a warmed platter. Garnish with the rosemary and thyme sprigs and serve immediately.

Serves 6–8

Crusted Rack of Lamb

2 tablespoons Dijon-style mustard

2 tablespoons olive oil

2 tablespoons fresh lemon juice

½ teaspoon salt, plus salt to taste

½ teaspoon freshly ground pepper,
   plus freshly ground pepper to taste

3 cups (6 oz/185 g) fresh herbed bread
   crumbs (recipe on page 14)

3 cloves garlic, minced

⅓ cup (⅓ oz/10 g) minced fresh mint

3 racks of lamb, about 1½ lb (750 g)
   each, trimmed (see note)

¼ cup (2 oz/60 g) unsalted butter,
   melted

Have your butcher trim off 2 inches (5 cm) of fat between each chop in the racks, exposing the tips of the rib bones. This is called "frenching" the racks. Accompany with tiny roasted red potatoes and a medley of seasonal fresh vegetables such as asparagus, sugar snap peas and carrots.

*P*osition a rack in the middle of an oven and preheat to 400°F (200°C).

In a small bowl, whisk together the mustard, olive oil, lemon juice and the ½ teaspoon each salt and pepper. Set aside.

In a food processor fitted with the metal blade, combine the bread crumbs, garlic, mint, and salt and pepper to taste. Process until well mixed. Set aside.

Lay the racks of lamb in a roasting pan, side by side and fat side up. Roast on the middle rack for 10 minutes. Remove from the oven and immediately rub the mustard mixture on the top of the lamb. Then spread the bread crumb mixture evenly on the mustard. Drizzle the melted butter evenly over the bread crumbs and return the lamb to the oven.

Continue to roast the lamb until the crumbs are golden and an instant-read thermometer inserted into the thickest portion of a rack away from the bone registers 130°–135°F (54°–57°C) for medium-rare or the meat is pink when cut with a sharp knife, about 20 minutes longer. Transfer the lamb to a cutting board and cover with aluminum foil. Let rest for 10 minutes before carving.

Slice the lamb between the ribs and arrange 2 or 3 ribs on each warmed plate. Serve immediately.

Serves 6

Spiced Lamb Meatballs with Tomatoes and Cilantro

FOR THE MEATBALLS:

1 lb (500 g) ground (minced) lamb
½ cup (2½ oz/75 g) finely minced
  yellow onion
2 cloves garlic, minced
4 tablespoons chopped fresh parsley
5 tablespoons chopped fresh cilantro
  (fresh coriander)
1 teaspoon ground cumin
1 teaspoon sweet paprika
¾ teaspoon ground ginger
¼ cup (2 oz/60 g) dried bread crumbs
  or dried herbed bread crumbs
  (recipe on page 14)
1 teaspoon salt
1 teaspoon freshly ground pepper
1 tablespoon olive oil

FOR THE TOMATO SAUCE:

3 cups (18 oz/560 g) peeled, seeded and
  chopped tomatoes (fresh or canned)
½ cup (2 oz/60 g) chopped yellow
  onion
2 cloves garlic, minced
¼ teaspoon crushed red pepper flakes
¼ cup (½ oz/15 g) chopped fresh
  cilantro (fresh coriander)
pinch of saffron threads
salt and freshly ground pepper

fresh cilantro (fresh coriander) sprigs

This fragrant dish is an adaptation of a Moroccan tagine, or slowly simmered stew. Accompany with steamed couscous and a hearty red wine.

*P*reheat an oven to 450°F (230°C).

To make the meatballs, in a bowl, combine the lamb, onion, garlic, parsley, cilantro, cumin, paprika, ginger, bread crumbs, salt and pepper. Form into balls about 1 inch (2.5 cm) in diameter. Grease a baking sheet with the olive oil and place the meatballs on it. Bake until brown, about 10 minutes. Remove from the oven and set aside.

To make the tomato sauce, in a blender or in a food processor fitted with the metal blade, combine the tomatoes, onion, garlic, red pepper flakes, cilantro, saffron, and salt and pepper to taste. Process until smooth. Pour the tomato sauce into a large frying pan or sauté pan set over medium-low heat. Bring to a simmer and cook, uncovered, until the sauce thickens, about 30 minutes.

Add the lamb meatballs to the sauce and continue to simmer gently, uncovered, until the lamb is cooked, 10–15 minutes.

To serve, transfer the meatballs and sauce to a large bowl. Garnish with the cilantro sprigs and serve immediately.

Serves 6

Lamb and Black Bean Chili

1½ cups (10½ oz/330 g) dried black
  beans
¼ cup (2 fl oz/60 ml) olive oil
2 lb (1 kg) boneless lamb cut from the
  leg or shoulder, trimmed of excess fat
  and cut into 1-inch (2.5-cm) cubes
2 yellow onions, chopped
1 green bell pepper (capsicum), seeded,
  deribbed and cut into ½-inch
  (12-mm) dice
2 or 3 fresh serrano or jalapeño chili
  peppers, minced
6 tablespoons chili powder
3 tablespoons ground cumin
5 large cloves garlic, minced
4 cups (1½ lb/750 g) peeled, seeded
  and chopped tomatoes (fresh or
  canned)
2 cups (16 fl oz/500 ml) beer or water
salt and freshly ground pepper

In the Southwest there are as many variations on chili as there are cooks. This one is especially tasty. Other dried beans, such as pinto beans, navy beans or cranberry beans, can be substituted for the black beans. Garnish the chili with sour cream, a mixture of grated Cheddar and Monterey Jack cheeses, chopped green (spring) onions, jalapeños, fresh cilantro (fresh coriander) and/or lime wedges. Serve warm flour tortillas or crispy fried corn tortilla chips on the side.

Pick over the beans and discard any stones; rinse well. Place in a bowl and add water to cover generously. Soak for at least 4 hours or as long as overnight.

Drain the beans and place them in a large saucepan. Add water to cover by 2 inches (5 cm). Bring to a boil, reduce the heat to low and simmer, uncovered, until the beans are almost cooked, about 30 minutes. Remove from the heat. Drain, reserving the cooking liquid. Set the beans and liquid aside separately.

In a large soup pot over medium-high heat, warm the olive oil. Working in batches if necessary, add the lamb cubes in a single layer (do not crowd the pot) and brown on all sides, about 10 minutes. Using a slotted spoon, transfer the lamb to a plate.

Reduce the heat to low and add the onions, bell pepper, chili peppers, chili powder and cumin and sauté, stirring, until the onions are soft, about 10 minutes. Add the garlic and sauté, stirring, for 2 minutes. Return the lamb to the pot and add the beans and their liquid, the tomatoes and beer or water. Simmer gently, uncovered, until the beans and lamb are very tender, 2½–3 hours, adding a little water if the mixture becomes too dry.

Season to taste with salt and pepper. Ladle into warmed bowls and serve immediately.

Serves 6

Turkish Spiced Lamb and Tomato Pizza

FOR THE TOPPING:

2 tablespoons olive oil

1 small yellow onion, finely chopped

6 oz (185 g) ground (minced) lamb

2 small tomatoes, finely chopped

1½ tablespoons tomato paste

1½ tablespoons chopped fresh parsley

3 tablespoons pine nuts

¼ teaspoon ground cinnamon

¼ teaspoon ground allspice

¼ teaspoon cayenne pepper

salt and freshly ground black pepper

6 oz (185 g) mozzarella cheese, shredded

1 partially baked, ready-made 12-inch (30-cm) pizza crust or ½ lb (250 g) pizza dough

If you prefer, make your own favorite pizza dough recipe for this Turkish-inspired pie. Fontina cheese or an equal combination of Fontina and mozzarella can be used in place of mozzarella for added flavor. The spiced lamb would make a great filling for an omelet or a topping for pasta.

Preheat an oven to 500°F (260°C).

To make the topping, in a large frying pan or sauté pan over low heat, warm the olive oil. Add the onion and sauté, stirring, until soft, about 10 minutes. Crumble the lamb into the pan and add the tomatoes, tomato paste, parsley, pine nuts, cinnamon, allspice, cayenne pepper, and salt and black pepper to taste. Cook gently, uncovered, until the mixture is almost dry, about 10 minutes.

Place the pizza crust on a baking sheet. If using pizza dough, roll it out on a floured work surface into a 12-inch (30-cm) round and transfer it to an oiled baking sheet.

Scatter the cheese on top of the pizza round, leaving a 1-inch (2.5-cm) border uncovered around the edge. Distribute the lamb mixture evenly over the cheese. Bake until the cheese melts and the crust is crispy and golden, 6–8 minutes if using a partially baked crust or 10–12 minutes if using pizza dough.

Remove from the oven, cut into wedges and serve at once.

Serves 6 as an appetizer or 2 as a main course

Salad of Grilled Lamb, Potatoes and Garlic Mayonnaise

2 lb (1 kg) small red potatoes, unpeeled
  and well scrubbed
2 tablespoons olive oil
salt and freshly ground pepper

FOR THE GARLIC MAYONNAISE:
1 egg yolk
1 teaspoon Dijon-style mustard
⅓ cup (3 fl oz/80 ml) olive oil
⅓ cup (3 fl oz/80 ml) vegetable oil
juice of ½ lemon
2 or 3 cloves garlic, minced
salt and freshly ground pepper
2 tablespoons warm water

3–3¼ lb (1.5–1.65 kg) leg of lamb,
  trimmed of excess fat, boned and
  butterflied (see page 11)
2 tablespoons olive oil
salt and freshly ground pepper
3 red bell peppers (capsicums), roasted
  (see glossary, page 104) and cut
  lengthwise into strips 1 inch
  (2.5 cm) wide (optional)
fresh parsley leaves, preferably flat-leaf
  (Italian)

Preheat an oven to 375°F (190°C). Prepare a fire in a charcoal grill.

Place the potatoes in a single layer in a baking dish. Add the oil and salt and pepper to taste and turn the potatoes to coat them evenly. Cover with aluminum foil and bake until tender, 40–50 minutes. Remove from the oven and remove the foil.

Meanwhile, make the garlic mayonnaise: In a bowl, whisk together the egg yolk, mustard and 1 tablespoon of the olive oil until an emulsion forms. In a cup, combine the remaining olive oil and the vegetable oil. Whisking constantly, gradually add the oils until the emulsion thickens. Add the lemon juice, garlic, and salt and pepper to taste. Whisk in the warm water to make the mayonnaise barely fluid. Cover and refrigerate.

Rub the lamb with the olive oil and salt and pepper to taste. About 10 minutes after placing the potatoes in the oven, place the lamb on the grill rack 4 inches (10 cm) from the heat source and grill until the first side is golden brown, about 15 minutes. Turn over the lamb and continue to cook until an instant-read thermometer inserted into the thickest portion registers 130°–135°F (54°–57°C) for medium-rare or the meat is pink when cut with a sharp knife, about 15 minutes longer. Transfer to a cutting board and cover with aluminum foil. Let rest for 10 minutes before carving.

Meanwhile, place the potatoes on the grill rack and grill, turning occasionally, until hot and well marked, about 10 minutes.

Cut the lamb across the grain into thin slices and arrange on a platter with the potatoes and the roasted bell peppers, if using. Garnish with parsley and serve the garlic mayonnaise on the side.

Serves 6

Glossary

The following glossary defines terms both generally and specifically as they relate to pork and lamb, including major and unusual ingredients and basic techniques.

ALLSPICE
Sweet spice of Caribbean origin with a flavor suggesting a blend of cinnamon, cloves and **nutmeg.**

BAY LEAVES
Dried whole leaves of the bay laurel tree. Pungent and spicy, they flavor simmered dishes, marinades and pickling mixtures.

BEANS AND LENTILS
Many kinds of dried beans and lentils are often used in meat stews or braises. Before use, dried beans and lentils should be carefully picked over to remove any impurities such as small stones or fibers or any discolored or misshapen beans. To rehydrate beans and thus shorten their cooking time and improve their digestibility, they are often presoaked in cold water to cover generously for at least 4 hours or as long as overnight. The more common dried varieties used in this book include:

Black Beans
Earthy-tasting, mealy-textured beans, relatively small in size and with deep black skins. Also called turtle beans. Available canned as well.

Cannellini Beans
Italian variety of small to medium, white, thin-skinned, oval beans.

Great Northern or white (navy) beans may be substituted. Also available canned.

Kidney Beans
Popular, kidney-shaped beans with brownish red skins, slightly mealy texture and robust flavor. White kidney beans are also available.

Lentils
Small, disk-shaped dried legumes, prized for their rich, earthy flavor when cooked.

White (Navy) Beans
Small, white, thin-skinned oval beans. Also known as Boston beans. Great Northern beans may be substituted.

CAPERS
Small, pickled buds of a bush common to the Mediterranean, used whole as a savory flavoring or garnish.

CAYENNE PEPPER
Very hot ground spice derived from dried cayenne chili peppers.

CHILI PEPPERS
Any of a wide variety of peppers prized for the mild-to-hot spiciness they impart as a seasoning. Two of the most common fresh green varieties, used in this book, are the small, thick-fleshed, fiery jalapeño (below, left) and the small, slender, even hotter serrano (below, right).

When handling any chili, wear kitchen gloves to prevent any cuts or abrasions on your hands from contacting the pepper's volatile oils. Afterwards, wash your hands well with warm, soapy water, and take special care not to touch your eyes or any other sensitive areas.

BELL PEPPER
Fresh, sweet-fleshed, bell-shaped member of the pepper family. Also known as capsicum. Most common in the unripe green form, although ripened red or yellow varieties are also available. Creamy pale-yellow, orange and purple-black types may also be found.

To prepare a raw bell pepper, cut it in half lengthwise with a sharp knife. Pull out the stem section from each half, along with the cluster of seeds attached to it.

Remove any remaining seeds, along with any thin white membranes, or ribs, to which they are attached.

Cut the pepper halves into quarters, strips or slices, or as directed in specific recipes.

When a recipe calls for roasted and peeled bell peppers, preheat a broiler (griller). Cut the bell peppers in half lengthwise and remove the stems, seeds and ribs as directed above. Place the pepper halves on a broiler pan, cut side down, and broil until the skins blister and turn black. Transfer to a paper or plastic bag and let stand until the peppers soften, about 10 minutes. Using your fingertips or a small knife, peel off the blackened skins. Then tear or cut the peppers as directed in the recipe.

CILANTRO
Green, leafy herb resembling flat-leaf (Italian) **parsley,** with a sharp, aromatic, somewhat astringent flavor. Popular in Latin American and Asian cuisines. Also called fresh **coriander** and commonly referred to as Chinese parsley.

COCONUT MILK
Although commonly thought to be the thin, relatively clear liquid found inside a whole coconut, coconut milk is actually an extract made from shredded fresh coconut. Unsweetened coconut milk is available in cans in Asian markets and well-stocked food stores.

CORIANDER
Small, spicy-sweet seeds of the coriander plant, which is also called **cilantro** or Chinese parsley.

CORNSTARCH
Fine, powdery flour ground from the endosperm of corn—the white heart of the kernel—and, because it contains no gluten, used as a thickening agent in some sauces, stir-fries and stews. Also known as cornflour.

CUMIN
Middle Eastern spice with a strong, dusky, aromatic flavor. Sold either ground or as whole, small, crescent-shaped seeds.

CURRY POWDER
A blend of spices commonly used to flavor East Indian–style dishes. Most curry powders will include **coriander, cumin,** chili powder, fenugreek and turmeric; other additions may include cardamom, cinnamon, cloves, **allspice,** fennel seeds and **ginger.**

EGGPLANT

Vegetable-fruit, also known as aubergine, with tender, mildly earthy, sweet flesh. The shiny skins of eggplants vary in color from purple to red and from yellow to white, and their shapes range from small and oval to long and slender to large and pear shaped. The most common variety is the large, purple globe eggplant. Slender, purple Asian eggplants (below), more tender and with fewer, smaller seeds, are available with increasing frequency in food stores and vegetable markets.

FISH SAUCE

Popular Southeast Asian seasoning prepared from salted, fermented fish, usually anchovies. Also known as *nuoc mam* (Vietnamese), *nam pla* (Thai) and *patis* (Filipino).

GINGER

The rhizome of the tropical ginger plant, which yields a sweet, strong-flavored spice. Whole ginger rhizomes, commonly but mistakenly called roots, may be purchased fresh in a food store or vegetable market.

HOT-PEPPER SAUCE

Bottled commercial cooking and table sauce made from fresh or dried hot red **chili peppers.** Tabasco is the most commonly known brand.

MAPLE SYRUP

Syrup made from boiling the sap of the maple tree. It has an inimitably rich savor, intense sweetness and deep caramel color.

MUSTARDS

Dijon mustard is made in Dijon, France, from brown mustard seeds (unless marked *blanc*) and white wine or wine vinegar. Pale in color, fairly hot and sharp tasting, true Dijon mustard and non-French blends labeled "Dijon-style" are widely available. Coarse-grained mustards, which have a granular texture due to roughly ground mustard seeds, include the French moutarde de Meaux and some high-quality British and German varieties.

NUTMEG

Sweet spice that is the hard pit of the fruit of the nutmeg tree. May be bought already ground or, for fresher flavor, whole. Whole nutmegs may be kept inside special nutmeg graters (below), which include hinged flaps that conceal a storage compartment, and grated as needed.

OILS

Oils not only provide a medium in which foods may be browned without sticking, but can also subtly enhance the flavor of many dishes. Store in airtight containers away from heat and light.

Extra-virgin olive oil, extracted from olives on the first pressing without use of heat or chemicals, is prized for its pure, fruity taste and golden to pale green hue. The higher-priced extra-virgin olive oils are usually of better quality. Products labeled "pure olive oil," less aromatic and flavorful, may be used for all-purpose cooking.

Pale gold peanut oil has a subtle hint of the peanut's richness.

Rich and flavorful sesame oil is pressed from sesame seeds. Sesame oils from China and Japan are made with toasted sesame seeds, resulting in a dark, strong oil used primarily as a flavoring ingredient.

LAMB

Lamb destined for the market is first divided into large primal or wholesale cuts that are then cut into the individual retail cuts sold in markets. Some cuts may not be commonly available in some food stores and should be sought from a quality butcher. This silhouetted illustration shows the standard American primal cuts; individual retail cuts used in this book are included in the text that follows.

Neck (A)

Meat from the neck section, rich in flavor but tough, is most commonly sold ground (minced).

Shoulder (B)

Meat from the shoulder, flavorful and moderately fatty, yields chops, cubes of stewing and kebab meat, and ground (minced) lamb, as well as rolled boned roasts.

Rib (C)

With its rich, tender meat, the rib section yields lamb chops for sautéing, broiling or grilling, as well as the whole rib roast known as a rack of lamb.

Loin & Flank (D)

Very tender loin meat is the source of the tenderloin and loin chops for broiling, grilling or sautéing, as well as whole roasts. Tough but flavorful flank meat is most often ground (minced).

Saddle (E)

The lamb's saddle portion contains the sirloin, which may be roasted whole or cut into chops or steaks for grilling, broiling or sautéing.

Leg (F)

The firm, flavorful leg meat may be roasted whole or boned, or cut into cubes for kebabs or stew.

Foreshank & Hindshank (G)

The small, lean foreshank is usually braised as an individual-serving cut. The hind shank may be cut into thick crosswise slices for braising—the classic *ossobuco* of Italy—or it may be boned and cut into stew meat.

Breast (H)

This section of fatty, flavorful meat, with its many tiny rib bones, may be cooked whole by braising or roasting; cut up and braised as lamb riblets; or boned and ground (minced).

Walnut and hazelnut oils are reminiscent of the flavor of the nuts from which they were pressed.

Flavorless vegetable and seed oils such as safflower, canola and corn oil are employed for their high cooking temperatures and bland flavor.

OLIVES
Throughout Mediterranean Europe, ripe black olives are cured in combinations of salt, seasonings, brines, vinegars and oils to produce pungently flavored results. Good-quality cured olives, such as French Niçoise (below, right), Greek Kalamata (below, left) or Italian Gaeta, are available in ethnic delicatessens, specialty-food shops and well-stocked food stores.

OREGANO
Aromatic, pungent and spicy Mediterranean herb—also known as wild marjoram—used fresh or dried as a seasoning for all kinds of savory dishes. Especially popular in dishes featuring tomatoes and other vegetables.

PAPRIKA
Powdered spice derived from the dried paprika pepper; popular in several European cuisines and available in sweet, mild and hot forms. Hungarian paprika is the best, but Spanish paprika, which is mild, may also be used.

PARMESAN CHEESE
Firm, hard-crusted Italian cow's milk cheese with a sharp, salty, full flavor resulting from up to 2 years of aging. Buy in block form, to grate fresh as needed (see below), rather than already grated. The finest Italian variety is designated Parmigiano-Reggiano.®

PARSLEY
This widely used fresh herb is available in two varieties: the more popular curly-leaf type and a flat-leaf type, known as Italian parsley, which resembles **cilantro.** Relatively tough parsley stems, although usually discarded, may also be used to add the herb's flavor to long-simmered dishes.

PECANS
Brown-skinned, crinkly textured nuts with a distinctive sweet, rich flavor and crisp texture.

PINE NUTS
Small, ivory seeds extracted from the cones of a species of pine tree, with a rich, slightly resinous flavor (below).

RED PEPPER FLAKES
Coarsely ground flakes of dried red chilies, including seeds, which add moderately hot flavor to the foods they season.

RICE
Among the many varieties of rice available around the world are the popular long-grain white rice, a

PORK
Before it is cut into individual retail cuts, pork is first divided into the large primal or wholesale cuts shown in the silhouetted illustration below. Individual retail cuts used in this book are discussed in the text that follows; some cuts may not be commonly available and should be sought from a quality butcher.

Shoulder (A)
This tough, meaty primal cut yields bone-in and boneless shoulder roasts. The boned meat may also be cut into cubes for grilled or broiled kebabs, or it may be chopped for ground (minced) pork or sausage.

Blade and Center Loin (B)
The front blade section of the loin, with its rich, tender meat, is cut into large blade roasts or sliced into bone-in blade chops. Toward the center of the loin, the meat becomes juicier and more tender still. It may be cut into chops for grilling, broiling or sautéing; and a section with rib bones attached may be shaped and tied into the descriptively named crown roast. The tender back ribs from this section are excellent for barbecuing.

Sirloin (C)
The tenderest pork of all, the tenderloin, comes from this primal cut. The thin tenderloin may be grilled, broiled or sautéed whole, or cut into thin scallops for sautéing. Loin chops may also be cut from this section for grilling, broiling or sautéing.

Ham (D)
The ham section is the source of bone-in, partially boned and boneless hams. Of these, a country-style ham refers to one that has been cured with salt or brine and other seasonings, then smoked; the ham is then usually cooked partially or completely before sale. The fine-grained meat from the center of this section may also be cut to make ham steaks. The top, or butt, portion, which is almost boneless, may also be roasted or braised.

Belly (E)
With their very tender meat and generous amounts of fat, the rib bones from the front portion of this primal cut become pork spareribs for baking or grilling. The remainder of the belly yields bacon or salt pork.

Feet (F)
Also known as trotters. Sometimes used as a rich source of gelatin for flavoring and thickening stocks and stews.

slender variety from which the brown bran has been polished to yield separate, full grains when cooked, and basmati, a particular type of long-grain white rice that cooks to form fluffy, fragrant individual kernels. Wild rice is, in fact, unrelated to rice; a wild grain native to Minnesota, its unpolished dark brown kernels have a rich flavor and texture that are oftened compared to that of nuts.

ROSEMARY
Mediterranean herb, used either fresh or dried, with a strong aromatic flavor well suited to pork and lamb dishes.

SAFFRON
Intensely aromatic spice, golden orange in color, made from the dried stigmas of a species of crocus; used to perfume and color many classic Mediterranean and East Indian dishes. Sold either as threads—the dried stigmas—or in powdered form. Look for products labeled "pure" saffron.

SOY SAUCE
Asian seasoning and condiment made from soybeans, wheat, salt and water. Seek out good-quality imported soy sauces; Chinese brands tend to be markedly saltier than Japanese. Those labeled "dark" soy sauce have a fuller, richer flavor.

THYME
Fragrant, clean-tasting, small-leaved herb popular as a seasoning for light meats, poultry, seafood or vegetables. Use fresh or dried.

TOMATOES
During summer, when tomatoes are in season, use the best red or yellow sun-ripened tomatoes you can find. At other times of year, plum tomatoes, sometimes called Roma or egg tomatoes, are likely to have the best flavor and texture; canned whole plum tomatoes are also good. Small red or yellow cherry tomatoes, barely bigger than the fruit for which they are descriptively named, also have a pronounced flavor that makes them an ideal candidate for use fresh or in cooked dishes during their peak summer season.

Peeling Fresh Tomatoes
To peel fresh tomatoes, bring a saucepan three-fourths full of water to a boil. Using a small, sharp knife, cut out the core from the stem end of the tomato. Then cut a shallow X in the skin at the tomato's base. Submerge for about 20 seconds in the boiling water, then remove and dip in a bowl of cold water. Starting at the X, peel the skin from the tomato, using your fingertips and, if necessary, the knife blade.

TOMATILLOS
The small green tomatillo resembles but is not actually related to the tomato. Fresh tomatillos, available in some Latin American markets and well-stocked food stores, usually come encased in brown papery husks, easily peeled off before tomatillos are cut. Canned tomatillos may be found in specialty-food sections of most markets.

TOMATO PASTE
A commercial concentrate of puréed tomatoes, used to add flavor and body to sauces. Often sold in small cans. Imported tubes of double-strength tomato concentrate, sold in Italian delicatessens and well-stocked food markets, have a superior flavor.

TOMATO PURÉE
Good-quality canned tomato purées are available in most markets. To make your own tomato purée, peel and seed the **tomatoes,** then purée in a blender or a food processor fitted with the metal blade.

TOMATOES, SUN-DRIED
When sliced crosswise or halved and then dried in the sun, tomatoes develop an intense, sweet-tart flavor and a pleasantly chewy texture that enhance savory recipes. Available either packed in oil or dry.

VINEGARS
Literally "sour wine," vinegar results when certain strains of yeast cause wine or some other alcoholic liquid such as apple cider or Japanese rice wine to ferment for a second time, turning it acidic. The best-quality wine vinegars begin with good-quality

wine. Red wine vinegar, like the wine from which it is made, has a more robust flavor than vinegar produced from white wine. Balsamic vinegar, a specialty of Modena, Italy, is a vinegar made from reduced grape juice and aged for many years. Sherry vinegar has its own rich flavor and color reminiscent of the fortified, cask-aged aperitif wine. Cider vinegar has the sweet tang and golden color of the apple cider from which it is made. Rice wine vinegar, a specialty of Japan, possesses a delicacy that suits it well to Asian dishes.

WORCESTERSHIRE SAUCE
Traditional English seasoning or condiment; an intensely flavorful, savory and aromatic blend of many ingredients, including molasses, **soy sauce,** garlic, onion and anchovies. Popular as a marinade ingredient or table sauce for grilled foods, especially red meats.

ZEST
Thin, brightly colored, outermost layer of a citrus fruit's peel, containing most of its aromatic essential oils—a lively source of flavor. Zest may be removed with a simple tool known as a zester, drawn across the fruit's skin to remove the zest in thin strips (see below); with a fine hand-held grater; or in wide strips with a vegetable peeler or a paring knife held almost parallel to the fruit's skin. Zest removed with the latter two tools may then be thinly sliced or chopped on a cutting board.

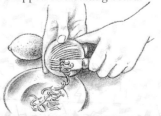

Index

⭐

ACKNOWLEDGMENTS

The publishers would like to thank the following people and organizations
for their generous assistance and support in producing this book:
Jean Tenanes, Anita Anderson, Jinny Harubin, Jeff Alexson, Paul Weir, Sharon C. Lott, Jim Obata,
Stephen W. Griswold, Ken DellaPenta, Claire Sanchez, Stephani Grant, Jennifer Mullins,
and the buyers and store managers for Pottery Barn and Williams-Sonoma stores.

The following kindly lent props for the photography: Biordi Art Imports, Candelier,
Fillamento, Forrest Jones, Sue Fisher King, RH Shop and Chuck Williams.